Getting Along With People Is EASY!

By Wayne Kehl

authorHOUSE®

AuthorHouse™
1663 Liberty Drive, Suite 200
Bloomington, IN 47403
www.authorhouse.com
Phone: 1-800-839-8640

First published by AuthorHouse 1/5/2009

ISBN: 978-1-4389-3723-6 (sc)

Printed in the United States of America
Bloomington, Indiana

This book is printed on acid-free paper.

Getting Along With People Is EASY!

Arrogance
Honesty
Distrust
Greed
Humility
Enthusiasm
Integrity
Awareness
Humor
Conceited
Angry
Secrecy
Sullen
Reticent
Underhanded
Competitive
Pretentious
Self esteem
Kindness
Culture
Religion
Race
Shy
Gender
Prejudice
Egotistical
Sincere
Discriminatory
Lazy
Industrious
Overbearing
Positive

EASY!

A guide to understanding relationships, along with some good advice that will make your life better!

Table of Contents

Foreword

As I kneeled to thin out the dead stalks in the rose bushes near my back gate today, I felt a twinge in my back. As I stood up to shake off the twinge, I felt a pain in my right thigh and stiffness in both knees. At that moment, I mumbled silently to myself, "Is this what life is all about?" I realized at that moment that I was feeling my age and things that seemed easy to me in my youth would slowly but surely become more difficult with the passing years. Eventually, one by one, things that I have until now taken for granted, will become impossible. The aging process will progress resolutely until the day of my ultimate passing from this wonderful life. Loss of youth is frustrating but not nearly so daunting as the final curtain and the realization that when my life-light goes out, all that will survive are the memories others have of me. Since I can't hold the curtain back forever, I want those memories to be predominantly pleasurable for those who outlive me.

If I live to the age of eighty, I will have lived slightly more than twenty nine thousand days. At this moment, still assuming I will live until I am eighty, I have approximately nine thousand days left. It is at this point in one's life that almost involuntarily, a grand reassessment begins. I know what I have done so far in my life and I know which bits of it added value to others, and to myself. I am aware of the good that I have done and I am grudgingly conscious of the bad. In this last third of my earthly existence, I wonder what my future purpose is. What shall I do? Should I become a recluse and hide from all of the problems of the people who annoy me? Shall I spend the balance of my earthly sentence thinning roses and mowing the lawn, oblivious to the world outside…or, alternatively, should I become a supporter of causes that help other people while working tirelessly to make the world a better place? All have their benefits and all appeal to me in their own unique ways. The wonderful glory of these options is that I have choices. I can do whatever I want. That is the beauty of being human and living free.

One choice I have made is to awake on every one of my last nine thousand mornings with a smile on my face. Every day I have had until now has been a privilege and every day I have from this day forward will be a precious gift. I have come to the irrefutable conclusion that I cannot keep my smile alive without the help of other people. If the folks in the world who are going to join me in my last nine thousand days do not share my dream of daily happiness, I will fail. When you have only nine thousand days to live, you tend to want to make the best of them. With that in mind, I intend to make sure the other folks on my nine thousand day odyssey, only see the best of me. If I get along with them, they will want me to be happy. If they enjoy my presence, they will do everything they can to make me smile. If I make their lives as pleasurable as I possibly can, they will reward me with kindness. In short, selfishly I intend to get along with everyone I meet. It will take a modicum of extra effort, but it will be worth it. The alternative is not getting along with other people, but that surely will not bring a smile to my face…or theirs.

Life is all about options and choices. I choose a life of fulfillment and joy. I choose getting along with people… I choose happiness! You can too!

Wayne Kehl

Introduction

As I passed through the first fifty years of my life, I noticed that each person I met was different; so different in fact that I found it almost impossible to guess what they might be thinking at any time or what their reactions might be to any given situation. Because of my inability to *read* other people or predict their actions and reactions, I found myself annoyed, angry, depressed, confused, disappointed, and even completely dumbfounded with people from time to time. Sometimes I took things one step further and used those emotions as reasons, excuses, or justifications to belittle people, avoid people, yell at people, or practice passive-aggressive behavior toward perfectly innocent people. The problems I had with them really had nothing to do with them. The problems I had with them were a result of my inability to control my own emotions and accept those people for who they were. Until now, I could not see that the problems I had with other people were in fact my own, and that I was singularly responsible for the fact that I did not get along with everyone I met. When faced with the challenge of not understanding other people, I chose to become difficult and to direct one form or another of negative behavior toward them.

My first half-century taught me that I knew very little about the inner feelings of others. Their thoughts, hopes, dreams, aspirations, and motivations were not only hidden from me, but I did little or nothing to find out what they might be. I did not try to put myself into their shoes or attempt to think the way they might have been thinking at any given time. I had not looked up the word *empathy* in the dictionary because I had no use for it. I did not try to see other perspectives because I generally assumed that my view of the world was the correct one. When I did not get along with people I assumed that it was their fault. At some point I even made an agreement with myself that it was okay for me to not get along with certain people simply because I had the right to be right. Occasionally I would even tell myself that these other people were missing out on a great thing by choosing not to get along with me.

I must point out at this juncture that as much as I did not get along with some people, I did get along with many others. As I was writing my first two books on leadership I came to the conclusion that even though I had a huge group of people in my life that I could legitimately call friends, I thought little about those good relationships. I tended to take them for granted. It was easy for me to get along with them. I gave no thought to what, if anything might be wrong or right with those relationships; I just accepted them for what they were and relied on them to always be there for me. The friendship of those people seemed unconditional and I believed that they would not, or could not, do me any harm. It finally occurred to me that I had been missing out on a huge opportunity for even more friendship and greater happiness in my life by limiting myself to my select group of friends. The people who were my friends were simply *easy*. They offered no threat to me and they accepted me for what I was. We struck a chord in each other that caused us to be attracted to one another. That realization led me to want to find out more about the segment of the population that I did not get along with. That search led me to this book.

In order to be able to speak competently about getting along with people I read everything I could get my hands on that dealt with human relationships. I also studied for and achieved the designations: Certified Professional Behavioral Analyst, Certified Professional Values Analyst and Certified Professional TriMetrix Analyst from Target Training International ©. Those certifications provided me solid scientific insight into the study of personal interests, attitudes, values, behavior, natural skills and the internal versus external emotional balance of human beings. As much as those studies were invaluable to me, the most telling research I did was out in the field…I talked to people, I observed people, and most importantly, I listened to people. People love to talk about themselves and if you simply ask them what they are thinking, they will probably tell you. *Asking* takes a bit of courage and intestinal fortitude, but it is the best way to get to the root of any situation and locate the real truth.

In these pages, you will find a myriad of human relationship scenarios along with positive and negative methods of dealing with them. My goal is to help you come to the realization that it is possible to get along with virtually anyone if you make the choice to do so. If you choose a positive response to all people no matter what their approach, your positive energy will be returned in kind.

Choose to be positive at all times and you will surely succeed. It's up to you!

I hope you enjoy, **"Getting Along With People Is EASY!"**

Wayne Kehl

www.waynekehl.com

CHAPTER ONE
Human Beings Are Born To Fight!

"Since the dawn of mankind, very few years have passed without a war somewhere in the world."

CHAPTER 1

As I prepared myself to write a book about people getting along with each other, I had to consider whether or not it mattered to most human beings whether they got along or not. I found myself wondering if it was possible that the general nature of people is so warped that they would prefer not to get along with each other. It was easy to find plenty of evidence that people *seem* to favor discord to harmony in their personal relationships. Everywhere I went I found people arguing, fighting, breaking up, breaking down, insulting each other, and threatening to sue each other. Conversely I found endless numbers of books, articles, television shows, personal coaches, religious leaders and psychologists devoted to the notion of bringing people together in a sort of worldwide love-in of compassion, kindness, empathy, sympathy, and soft heartedness. The business of helping folks to get along with other folks has become a multi-billion dollar industry that shows no signs of diminishing in the near future…and yet, people keep arguing and wars continue to rage!

IS IT POSSIBLE THAT MANKIND IS BEYOND HELP?

Is it possible that mankind is beyond help? Is all of the talk we hear about living kinder, gentler lives just a pipedream? Do you ever wonder if after you have seen your marriage counselor to sort out your differences with your spouse, your counselor goes home and lays a few carefully chosen degrading insults upon her own spouse in order to win an argument that began several years prior? Is it possible that your psychiatrist has anger management problems and takes his frustrations out on his children in the most violent of ways? Some business coaches are so bad at relationships that they can't even get along with their own employees. How on earth can they competently teach you how to get along with yours? Is it possible that our nature is so conflictive and naturally violent that we will never see a world where people get along on a regular and consistent basis? I would like to think that the answer to the last question is a resounding *NO* but despite my inherent optimism, the subject merits a huge amount of deliberation. As much as most of us want to get along with everyone we meet, we all seem to have trouble making it happen on a consistent basis.

HUMAN BEINGS ARE NATURALLY FASCINATED BY CONFLICT AMONGST OTHER HUMAN BEINGS.

Drawings on the walls of caves in various parts of the world tell us that cavemen fought for survival. Later drawings tell us that more highly evolved groups of human beings fought with each other for territorial dominance. Even later drawings show the evolution of kings, queens, chiefs, and great warriors who lead their people into war. It is apparent that long before the invention of newspapers and television when the news had to be laboriously transcribed onto cave walls, mankind already had media reporters who were compelled to record conflict and

4

the atrocities of war! Human beings are naturally fascinated by conflict amongst other human beings. It seems that they have enjoyed speaking of it and recording its facts by whatever means they had at their disposal ever since they learned the wizardry and wonder of communication.

Recorded history shows us some very interesting paradoxes. The Bible for example contains the "Ten Commandments" whose message is that people should be good to each other at all times, and in all ways. And yet, we also find historical figures in the Bible whose lives were awash with conflict and war. The Bible *is* the consummate *Good Book* for civilization and yet in addition to giving us direction on how to live a good life, it points out that life amongst human beings is not always good. Jesus spent his life on earth serving people and doing good things, and yet the very people he most wanted to help chose to end his earthly life in a horrendous and most undignified way. Was the act of nailing Jesus to the cross, foreshadowing that mankind would resort to violence to resolve its differences for all eternity? Or, was the crucifixion recorded in the Bible as a warning to readers in successive centuries that violence is a very poor way to settle disagreements. If the latter was the intent, mankind has yet to comprehend that message in any meaningful way. We are still finding reasons to fight on a daily basis just as we did during biblical times. When I ponder this subject I have to ask, "My goodness, if you can't get along with Jesus, who can you get along with?"

I often wonder what the people in Germany were thinking when Hitler was doing his thing. For the most part, Adolf was somewhat ordinary as leaders go. He was a smallish man with a bad moustache and all he really wanted was world dominance. Heck, most politicians and military leaders want world dominance. There wouldn't be much future for a politician who wanted everyone in the world to do as well as him and his followers. (Selflessness on a world scale is reserved for peaceful folks like the Deli Lama, Mother Teresa, Gandhi, and Bono of the rock band U2.) It is the natural mindset of politicians and military leaders to want to win. In order to win, there must be a competition of some sort and that often takes the form of a war. Despite the holocaust and Hitler's disgusting attempts to eliminate every Jewish person he could find, there were a lot of folks supporting him. No leader ever became a leader unless a lot of people wanted to be led by him or her, so it follows that Hitler was not a solitary, isolated island of genocide-mentality. Fortunately, when the Allied forces stopped his war effort, they also stopped the holocaust. I have often wondered what would have happened if Hitler had won the war. Would the people he conquered have accepted genocide for every person of Jewish descent in the world, or would sanity have prevailed? If the Allies had not become allies and Hitler had systematically conquered every country on earth, would his personal form of insanity have become accepted culture throughout the world? Or alternatively, would the natural goodness that gurgles through the bloodstream of every sane human being have risen up and eliminated the Nazi scourge from the world just as surely as the Allied war effort did. Before you answer, remember that most of the people who supported Hitler were considered sane prior to the war and only became infamous after he began to move his mass atrocity across Europe. It is clear that normal, sane human beings can be led to the acceptance of mass murder if provided with the right stimuli or some compelling reasoning that they can identify with. The same phenomenon that allowed acceptance of the holocaust can cause groups of everyday people to form a riot, or groups of children to bully a weaker classmate. Is it possible that the river of goodness that runs through all sane humans has a stream of potential evil running along side of it? Is it possible that people cannot control their own negative thoughts and that other people can easily bring our latent bad behavior to the surface if and when they choose to? It is truly tragic that the only way we could eliminate the continued spread of Hitler's holocaust was to end the lives of a huge number of good, sane people when essentially only one insane, sociopath was responsible for the entire debacle. World War Two, like all wars provided evidence of both the good and bad in people. It was also the ultimate expression of people not getting along with other people for very poor reasons.

Korea, Vietnam, and Iraq are all sites of major conflicts between people. All were victims of the atrocities of war and all have been saturated with the blood of many innocent civilians and equally innocent military men and women. All of those wars started after World War Two and all were motivated and enabled by politicians. Clearly little was learned from the *Great War* other than military strategy. None of those wars were to save the planet and none were due to any sort of alien invasion. If we were all under attack from misshapen, multi-colored creatures with big heads that were transported here from Mars or Saturn, I would be better able to understand and accept the loss of life that wars inevitably incur. The wars in question were a result of differences of opinion amongst various earthbound, human politicians and all could easily have been avoided. If the river of human goodness had overwhelmed the stream of human evil in each of these cases, the politicians would have settled their differences in boardrooms and everyone on earth could have slept better and lived longer.

Before turning to the subject of people getting along with people on a general, daily basis, we have to consider how normally good, sane people can easily turn to violence and even acceptance of the taking of human life with comparatively little provocation. It is part of the essence of mankind that inherently, we like a fight and we hesitate to back down from one. We have millenniums of evolution and centuries of cultural imprinting to overcome before we can be truly peaceful. In the meantime, we need to be aware of our human shortcomings while striving for a better life for ourselves. Once we get that *down pat* and begin to rely more on communication than on confrontation, we will have time to impart as much joy and value to those around us as we possibly can. Once we become adept at being good on a deliberate and consistent basis, we will find that getting along with people is easy!

Even in day to day life, well removed from war, we have conflict. Almost everything we do contains some element of conflict. In our modern civilization we refer to it as competition. We call it that in order to give it the appearance of a slightly milder and more palatable activity. Of course competition can lead to pure conflict but it is usually nothing more than *playing* at conflict or war. Football for example, is a game of competition that does an amazing job of mimicking a battlefield. In the National Football League large men put on plastic helmets and body armor to throw or kick a ball, with the intention of making it go over an end zone line or through a goal post. Both teams line up facing each other and when a whistle is blown the quarterback runs away from the front line with the ball in his hand while his receiver runs forward into enemy territory to try to catch the ball. With luck, skill, and good blocking by the other players, the quarterback may be fortunate enough to throw it directly to the receiver before being tackled by the opposing players. While that is going on, armor clad men from the team that does not have the ball run as quickly as possible at men on the team that does have the ball with the intention of preventing them from moving it over the line. In the course of it all, large men are constantly throwing themselves at other large men, knocking them to the ground as violently as possible. People on both teams stand a great chance of being seriously injured due to the physical abuse they must endure during each and every competition and most have very short careers. Football is very much like two enemy battalions of medieval foot soldiers lining up with metallic helmets and heavy body armor on a remote field waiting for the command from their leader to run forward, swords in hand, to attack and kill each other in order to take control of the battlefield. As in football, there is a line that must be crossed in order to claim victory and in both cases, the combatants are virtually forbidden from showing fear or pain. As in football various soldiers may try to sneak into enemy territory by flanking the enemy and as in football, various stronger soldiers will block the enemy in order to allow the more stealthy members in their army to move forward on the field. As in football medieval foot soldiers generally had very short careers and serious injury on the field was common. Fortunately for our modern day combatants, fewer football players are killed during a game than their medieval counterparts. In both cases the adoring public cheers wildly when their team/army is victorious and in both cases they are extremely depressed when their side loses.

IN THE TWENTY FIRST CENTURY EVEN SIMPLE PERSONAL APPEARANCE HAS BECOME A MATTER OF COMPETITION.

Football is not the only example of competition mimicking war or conflict. Virtually all games that our children play are based on the concept of one human being *beating* another or a team of players working together to be victorious over another. Even the apparently innocuous *spelling bee* is a form of competition where young children are pitted against each other with the intention of one person emerging victorious. The children work hard to sharpen their skills just as soldiers sharpen their swords before a battle. The children practice their spelling tirelessly just as soldiers practice their sword fighting skills prior to a skirmish. Just as in medieval warfare, the children drop one by one until only the strongest has survived…And as in medieval times, survivors are crowned victorious with great fanfare and adulation from the assembled throng of well-wishers. As the old adage says, *"to the victor go the spoils."* The stakes for modern day children are not as grave as they were for medieval warriors but the need to win can run just as strong and the negative feelings they have toward their opponents can run just as deep. Whether we like it our not, despite our modern laptop computers and cell phones, mankind is still essentially as primitively competitive and vengeful as we were during the Stone Age. Only the manner and process of our conflicts has changed.

In the twenty-first century even simple personal appearance has become a matter of competition. Hence the preponderance of weight loss products, health clubs, cosmetics, hair restoratives and breast enhancement surgeries. People are determined to be *better* than other people at almost everything they do. People who avail themselves of appearance improving products and services will generally tell you that they are doing it for *themselves*. They want to convince you that it was a personal decision that has nothing to do with anyone but them. If they were to think a little more about their motives, they would realize that they want to be the best looking person on the planet and are seeking the attention and admiration of everyone they meet. Their decision to improve their appearance is clearly not the result of some lonely aesthetic need for solitary, hidden beauty. Unfortunately this need for incredible attractiveness leads to arrogance, insecurity, anger, disagreement, strife, conflict, competition, pain, and emotional trauma in someone everyday. Most importantly, this innate need for superiority prevents people from getting along with other people. Think about why you don't like someone. Often you will find that they have said or done something that you felt was intended to make them somehow better than you or that they in someway belittled or wronged you to their own benefit. I believe that if we delve into the real reasons for human disagreement and conflict we may be able to create a world where people get along with each other routinely at a grass roots level and a world where conflict is a thing of the past. We will never reach everyone but if the majority of us are enlightened, we can improve our world immeasurably. At the very least, if we are aware of the dynamics of human behavior and disagreement, we can improve the fabric and substance of our own lives.

I believe that all people on this planet have value and that there is absolutely no reason why I should not get along with each and every one of them. Okay, you caught me! There are a few folks in prisons and mental institutions that may not be quite so easy to get along with... at least while they are incarcerated. However if we take the time to understand most folks, we will enrich our lives tremendously and move ever-closer to that totally peaceful state that eastern religions refer to as Nirvana. As much as I believe we have ingrained, primeval traits that are difficult to overcome, I also believe that with awareness, diligence and hard work, we can overcome them and enjoy life, free from the stress and unhappiness caused by human relationships.

In the coming chapters we will take steps toward our goal of making getting along with people easier. When you have finished this book, I hope that many of the human relationship challenges you may have been facing when you started reading it will be much more transparent and easy to deal with.

What did we learn in Chapter One?

- Human Beings have been seeking out and finding conflict ever since the dawn of mankind.

- Human Beings have been recording and reporting the events surrounding conflict and war ever since they learned how to communicate.

- Human Beings do not learn from their mistakes. There have been very few, if any years since the dawn of mankind when there was not a war raging somewhere in the world.

- Many modern sports and children's games are modeled after the strategy and conflict of war.

- Modern sports and children's games generate the same sort of emotion and competitiveness as war.

- Natural human competitiveness is the reason for fighting and wars.

- Human competitiveness touches all areas of our lives.

- There is no reason why we cannot get along with everyone we meet if we try.

CHAPTER TWO

TRUST ME!

"The more you tell people about yourself, the more they will trust you. The more they trust you, the more they will like you."

CHAPTER 2

The people you most enjoy spending time with generally do not attempt to compete with you except in a playful or mutually agreeable way. In fact, people with whom you share common interests and who do not attempt to compete with you for status, position, or power, often become your best friends. Those are the long-term, great relationships that we all cherish. You love to say nice things about these people and your friendship with them may actually be a matter of personal pride.

There are other people in your life with which you may share a similar socio-economic level; perhaps you live in the same neighborhood; maybe they have the same interests as you, and for all intents and purposes are just like you…but you hate them! You can't stand them! If you see them walking toward you in a shopping mall, you duck into the nearest store and hide behind a display rack until they have passed so that you don't have to talk to them. When others speak of them in glowing terms, you grimace but when others speak of them negatively, you love to join in and give your perspective on just how horrible they really are. In the worst cases, you might engage them in a debate every time they speak, or you may enjoy putting them down to others, (or under your breath) every chance you get. Sometimes you just avoid them and treat them with disdain. No matter how you handle these people, it is evident to them and probably to others, that you simply don't like them. Often the people you hate will retaliate by hating you too. In those cases, you may end up having silent battles with them that can occasionally erupt into full-fledged, vitriolic arguments.

PEOPLE CAN BE CRUEL...DON'T YOU THINK?

In today's society we are really not required to explain to anyone in detail *why* we don't like someone in order to prove or justify our dislike. It is simply enough that we say that he is a stupid *jerk* or that she is a conniving little *tramp*. Isn't it interesting that we like to find gender-specific terms for folks we don't like? A jerk is usually a man and a tramp is always a woman...unless he is a hobo. Often the terms we use to devalue people refer vulgarly to the body parts of the gender of our victim. In worst case scenarios we may even refer to a person by the name of a body part of his or her opposing gender. When that happens it is clear that we are very serious about our disdain. People can be cruel...don't you think? It often appears that we have still not evolved very far beyond that blood soaked, medieval battlefield!

In many cases, those that we have selected as true friends will support us in our cause and we are then able to form a *clique* of people whose primary focus is to destroy the life of the jerk or tramp. At that point the jerk or tramp will be compelled to defend himself or herself and they too might assemble a *clique* in order to 'counter-hate' the first *clique*. Then, other *clique* members will begin to dislike each other and the magic of gossip will create falsely based scenarios of horrible things that the various members of the *cliques* have done to earn the hatred of the others. The next thing you know, several relationships may be destroyed along with the reputations of some very good people. This stuff goes on in offices, sports teams, families, and even in churches every day.

YOU WILL NEVER TRULY LIKE OR LOVE SOMEONE YOU DO NOT TRUST.

So what might be the cause of all of this? It is clear that the poor behavior that people display toward each other results from our human need for competition, but the immediate and effective cause for the initial poor relationship is often a lack of trust. You will never truly like or love someone you do not trust, nor will you be able to continue liking or loving someone if for some reason you stop trusting them. Hence, the startling world divorce rate and the need for the word *trust* in the English language. If people did not have trouble trusting each other, there would be no need for trust. Trust would be the simple, unconditional acceptance of the truth and value of everything that is said and done by everyone in the world. What a strange and wonderful world that would be!

Men and women enter into marriage with the good and pure belief that they will live together in harmony for the rest of their lives. Often inexplicably during the course of that lifelong obligation, one or both of the participants in the marriage will do *something* to shatter the trust of the other. Statistically one of the main causes of divorce or separation is continued problems with money. How can that be? Money is not a person. Money has no emotions nor does it have any intellectual ability to influence anyone to do anything. Money in and of itself is inanimate and lifeless. It does not move and it does not emit any sort of sound or vibration. How can lifeless paper, metal, and plastic cause two people to stop believing in the vows that bound them together for eternity? How can money elevate itself to the level of a relationship-ending entity? Money is nothing without the intellectual gymnastics of human beings. People give life to money and even though it cannot speak or breathe they actually make it larger than life. When a husband decides to use more money than his wife feels is reasonable or when one spouse utilizes money without letting the other spouse in on the uses for it trust becomes an issue. When one of the spouses believes that they cannot trust the other with money, they often take the stance that the lifelong vows of marriage have less tangible value than money. When belief in the significance of the vows breaks down, the marriage comes to an end. Because some humans believe that money is more important than almost anything other than life itself, they are willing to forgo their vows and separate from the person they truly loved the most on the day of their nuptials.

Lack of trust may simply be transference of the competitive nature of humans. An untrusting wife for example may believe that the money spent by the husband would have been better spent on her. It may also be that the man does not believe that the woman has earned the right to spend as much money as she does. Perhaps one spouse contributed more funds to the overall joint account and feels that the portion he or she withdraws should therefore be greater. All of these scenarios are examples of the competitive nature of people. If one spouse has no concern about how much of the couple's overall funds belong to him or her, there will be no reason for concern or conflict and the usual feelings of betrayal or distrust will have no reason to exist. A marriage without concern for money is much more likely to survive than one where money is the focal point.

Most importantly, spending money without communication or mutual agreement is a sure-fire way to hurt and alienate a marriage partner. If the situation persists, the marriage commitment will gradually deteriorate and ultimately that one problem will overwhelm the many good things that may be present in the marriage. In the end it will destroy the relationship and divorce will become the logical course of action. The simple solution to this potential problem is open, honest communication. Married folks who know what their spouse is doing with their money and agree on the uses for the money will not experience any problems in that area. Usually one party will have a different view of appropriate spending than the other, so some negotiation might have to occur. However, that negotiation is an opportunity for discussion and bonding which will often bring couples closer together. In fact, if they have equally poor judgment and squander all of their money, ending up penniless on the street, they probably won't separate because of the money. They were after all, equal partners in their financial failure so their blame is equal and in a strong relationship where trust abounds, the bankruptcy should actually present another opportunity to display their solidarity and devotion to their vows. Alternatively, with passionately competitive people, eventually one person will blame the other for the failure and the marriage will break down. Dispensation of blame is another example of human competition. Blaming makes one party feel superior to the other. The person laying the blame feels superior since all responsibility has been placed squarely on the shoulders of the other who is then diminished in value because of it. It will also drive the trust-knife deeper since the person being blamed will not trust the other to have their best interests at heart, and again the relationship will break down. Lack of trust leads to blame; blame leads to anger; anger leads to divorce. As you can see, trust is a slippery slope for married folks.

Trust outside of marriage is also difficult. Because we spend approximately a third of our lives at work, our offices and jobsites can be virtual minefields of potential disagreements just waiting for a chance to explode. Getting along with co-workers can be difficult because we have no real vested interest in them. We have no lifelong commitment to them and we generally do not spend nights and weekends with them. Despite that, poor relationships at work can have long ranging harmful effects on our overall psyches since we tend to carry the effects home with us.

I believe it is safe to say that a relationship is a relationship, is a relationship. In other words, when we strip away the responsibilities and obligations of marriage and the trappings of titles or status at work, one relationship with a human being is the same as any other. The obligations of the marriage vows or work responsibilities may color our outward reactions, but our initial feelings when trust is violated or respect is lost are the same. This is partly because we all have personalities that are formed by the joining of the DNA of our natural parents, with the traits, perceptions, and values gained through the experiences and events that occur during the course of our lives. In other words, approximately fifty percent of our personality is imparted to us naturally and unavoidably by our parents and the other fifty percent is learned. It is assumed by most experts that by the time we reach our mid to late teens, our values and behaviors will be set in our minds and only subtle changes are likely to occur from then until our eventual demise. I tend to favor that theory since in my second century on earth I view things in essentially the same way that I did in my first and second quarter centuries. I may take a slightly more reasoned view and think a little longer before passing judgment now, but for the most part I am motivated by the same things and I react in much the same fashion as I did when I was a young person. As I have all my life, I still get excited on Christmas morning. As I did when I was twenty, I still become impatient with slow drivers. I still become angry when my integrity is questioned and I still become annoyed when I whistle for my dog, Mikki and she looks up at me with a huge smile on her face that seems to say, "Not just now, Dad. I have things to sniff over here!" I don't suppose I will ever feel differently about any of those situations. They are *me*. However, I recognize that I have the ability to amend my resulting behavior to something that is more palatable to others or more culturally acceptable. When I consciously decide to behave differently to a known stimulus, I am working my behavior muscles. In turn, they will improve over time just as the muscles in my biceps improve each time I lift weights. Eventually my mind will take on a mental form of *muscle memory* that will cause me to exercise better judgment every time I am faced with a situation that makes me uncomfortable. Exercising your behavior muscles is one of the best ways to make getting along with people easier. Think good thoughts; say good words; do good things!

WHEN TRUST FAILS, LACK OF RESPECT IS NOT FAR BEHIND.

When faced with a decision or a challenge at work, or with a group of friends, all of the DNA and ingrained learned behavior we have at our disposal is brought to the fore. We must immediately begin to evaluate the situation at hand and decide on a course of action. That decision will be based largely on how much we trust the information we have received and how much trust we place in the bearer of the information. For example, if our boss tells us we must start work an hour earlier to increase production in order to meet a deadline, or alternatively, face a layoff, we have three choices: We can accept what he is saying unconditionally and come in early to get the order out; we can doubt what he is saying but come in early anyway; or we can reject what he is saying and refuse to come in early. Each response will generate a different reaction from management and each will be based on the level of trust we have in our boss and/or the company we work for. Firstly, we must ponder whether or not the deadline is real or if our boss has made the story up to improve production beyond the necessary benchmark. If that is our thought, it is clear that we don't trust him at all. If we believe that the deadline is real but that we could complete the order during our regular working hours, we don't trust his judgment. If we believe the boss is telling us the full and complete truth and that failure to produce the order on time will bring grave results, we trust him fully. The interesting thing is that the folks who trust the boss fully will also *like* him a lot more than those who don't trust him at all or those who simply don't trust his judgment. Those who don't trust his judgment probably don't trust his reactions either. Those who don't believe in the deadline, but show up early anyway, don't trust him enough to have faith in whether he will actually lay them off or let them stay.

They aren't taking any chances! Those who refuse to show up early, are actually showing a bit of trust because either they trust him not to lay them off or they trust that he will lay them off but they don't care. Trust in negative behavior or bad results will not usually lead to good relationships, however.

Those who don't trust the judgment of the boss have moved into another area of poor relationships: *lack of respect*. Chances are because this boss has let his workers down in the past, they no longer have respect for him because they cannot trust him to make good decisions. Lack of respect goes hand in hand with lack of trust and is often the result of repeated disappointments. When trust fails, lack of respect is not far behind. When trust and respect are both gone, the chance of a positive relationship is virtually eliminated unless remedial effort is undertaken. The challenge is in recognizing when respect is gone and having the courage to address it openly and honestly with the people we don't trust. Fear can prevent openness and when fear takes over our judgment is colored to the point where we may permit intolerable situations to exist in our lives. It is actually possible for people to feign apparent affection for someone they don't trust even though deep in the recesses of their emotional centers, they have no real use for that person at all.

NO ONE LIKES LIARS BUT EVERYONE LIKES TO TALK ABOUT THEM!

In all cases, whether it is a boss, a spouse, a friend or someone you meet in a shopping mall, the best way to ensure that trust is evident is to speak honestly. Always be open and *tell the truth, the whole truth, and nothing but the truth* just as you would in a court of law. The quickest way to have others lose trust in you is to get caught in a lie. Think about the feelings you had when you found someone close to you lying about something. Think of the outrage, the betrayal, and the pure emotional pain you felt when you relied on what someone said only to find out later that it was pure fabrication. Think of how primeval rage or desperate disappointment rushed to the surface of your psyche and settled on the person who lied to you. Your anger and dismay may be verbalized or internalized, but either way, they are very real and they cut to the depth of your soul. Imagine how people are feeling about you when you lie to them! Keep in mind too, that when one person catches you in a lie, they will probably want to talk to other people about it. In that event, unbeknownst to you, your reputation as a liar will surely be building. No one likes liars but everyone likes to talk about them!

For some people, lying is second nature. They may have grown up in an environment where they were ignored or where they had siblings who received the lion's share of the attention. That can create insecurity and a lack of self esteem that has the ability to drive normal people to abnormal thoughts. In a desperate attempt to glean their share of adulation, they will sometimes invent fantasies of great deeds and tremendous adventures. Some children, who have less capacity for learning than their peers, might resort to lying in order to create an image of success. If they are failing in math for example, they might make up stories of unfounded athletic prowess or of valuable personal possessions that they have actually only dreamed of owning. Their goal is to minimize the accomplishments of their more scholarly peers while maximizing their own fabulous, albeit fictitious, existence. Their ego-driven, competitive need will force them to *one-up* their more gifted friends by trying to convince anyone who will listen that in their imaginary life they are extremely important and admired by all.

If insecurity is too deeply ingrained, the lying habit can become pathological to the point that individuals might actually begin to believe the fantasies and adventures that they have lied about. They will tell their lies so emphatically and passionately that even the most skeptical of listeners will be compelled to consider that the stories might be true. They can be so engaged in their imaginary life that if they falsely accuse someone of a horrendous wrongdoing, they will begin to believe in that person's non-existent guilt so strongly that they will fight tooth and nail to make it so. Pathological liars have the propensity to cause grievous emotional harm or even destroy the lives of people they envy or see as a threat. Because of their overwhelming need to be recognized, they may actually feel satisfaction or joy when they cause their victims to suffer. Those are extreme cases and fortunately comparatively few people of that nature populate the world. However, if you come across one of them it is best to steer a wide course away from them.

I think it is safe to say at this juncture that *everyone* has told a *white lie* or two. I actually know a few people that I trust and like even though they exaggerate the truth during almost every conversation I have with them. I accept their lying as a need to be acknowledged. I know instinctively that they would not deliberately hurt me and therefore I cannot consider them to be pathological. They are simply suffering from some minor insecurity and are compelled to overcome it with minor lies. These are good people who have wandered only slightly off the trail of truth. They have not lost their way; they are just staggering a bit. Occasionally I will quietly advise those folks that

I am aware of a certain lie in an effort to let them know that they are somewhat transparent. I prefer not to emotionally harm people with insecurities by *calling them out* or exposing them in front of others, but I do believe it is appropriate to let them know confidentially that their exaggerations are visible to all. When faced with truth they will understand the value of truth. Getting along with people requires empathy and compassion. We must seek to understand the motives of the people we have relationships with before we condemn them. Only then will we discover how easy it is to get along with people.

I have believed for a very long time that the more you tell folks about yourself, the more they will trust you. It naturally follows that the more they trust you, the more they will like you. It usually becomes apparent early in a relationship that people are intrigued when you open your heart and tell them about your life in very specific terms. When you allow them to know about your hopes, your dreams, your failures, your fears, your loves, your hates and whatever else is in the depths of your psyche, they will believe that you must surely trust them to the core. Why else would you be willing to expose yourself so fully to them? Conversely, when you withhold personal information and remain aloof and secretive, trust can never be established. People who know nothing *about* another person generally feel nothing *for* that person. They simply don't know them well enough to love them or hate them so no relationship is allowed to exist at all.

A SECRET LIFE IS A LONELY LIFE.

Trust is attracted to trust, just as a magnet is attracted to iron. When you shower another person with trust, they experience inexplicable, enveloping warmth that draws them to you. When that occurs, they are compelled to trust you at least as much as you trust them. If they have the courage to open up about themselves and trust you with their innermost secrets, you will have the basis of a great relationship. After a period of time, the only thing that can shatter a relationship that is built on trust is betrayal by one or another of the parties to it. It is easy to get along with people if you show them that you trust them. Be overt about it. Tell them how frightened you are; tell them how happy you are; tell them how much you love them; tell them everything! A secret life is a lonely life. If you really want to get along with people, open up your life and savor the true joy that only great relationships with other human beings can bring!

Another element of behavior that can destroy trust is a lack of consistency. When the actions of a human being cannot be relied upon, those that must relate to them are cautious in feeling trust for them. If a boss changes his attitude toward his employees on a regular basis he will probably not be highly regarded in the workplace. If he is angry and critical one day and overly complimentary the next, his motives will not be trusted and the reasons for his change of attitude will be in question. Bosses who act inconsistently will not be considered good leaders no matter how honorable their intentions are. The same holds true in relationships with friends. If you appear to enjoy a discussion about certain things one day and are obviously offended by a similar conversation another day, your friends will wonder what you must be thinking and again your motives will not be trusted. If you laugh at a minor insult on a Friday and cry when a similar slight is offered on a Monday, the people around you will not be able to trust your reactions and will begin to pull away from you. If you say you like seafood one day and hate it the next, your trust quotient will diminish. In all of these cases, you might also create a reputation for dishonesty because those close to you will assume that at least one of the statements or attitudes you offered must be false. The term *wishy-washy* is applied to people who change their minds regularly. It is also applied disrespectfully to people whose actions and reactions cannot be trusted. Those who attract the greatest amount of trust and who are universally liked are reliable and consistent in everything they do. Consistent people are easy to get along with.

People are so attached to trust that if you are ever convicted of a crime, the people who knew you before you got caught will never trust you again. The judicial system likes to suggest that incarceration and rehabilitation will actually allow a convict to have a normal life when released. Of course, we know that is not true. Most of us would probably not put a convicted embezzler in charge of our banking and nobody in their right mind would allow a convicted child molester to babysit their kids. Crime is the ultimate betrayal of trust. Crime is so heinous that robbery, assault, and murder are actually considered crimes against all of humanity. Even though only a small number of people are victims of any one criminal, our entire society gangs up on each and every one of them to destroy their lives just as they have destroyed the lives of others. I would not suggest that it should be any other way, but it does indicate the massive depth of need that mankind has for honesty and trust. Because of this need, if you want to be trusted you must always conduct yourself in a manner that will hold you above reproach. In your day to day life never lie, never fib, never spread scurrilous rumors, and always act with consistency. Your actions must be driven by honesty and your motives must be wholesome and true if you want to get along with people.

What did we learn in Chapter Two?

- People can be cruel to each other when there is no trust in a relationship.

- Some people will form cliques to destroy the life of someone they don't like.

- You can never truly like or love someone you do not trust.

- Marriage break down is usually due to a betrayal of trust.

- Always think about your behavior and the consequences of it before you react.

- When trust fails, lack of respect is not far behind.

- Liars can never be trusted.

- The more you tell people about yourself, the more they will trust you.

- Trust is the basis of all good relationships.

CHAPTER THREE
I'M NOT IN THE MOOD!

*"My mood is a reflection of
my perception of reality."*

CHAPTER 3

What is a mood? How do we get moods? Why would we choose to have a bad mood when a good mood is much more enjoyable? Are we having a mood at all times or are there times when we are just ourselves with no mood at all? Regardless of the answers to those questions, it is apparent that moods have a lot to do with how well people get along with each other.

Here is how dictionaries define the word, mood:

A conscious state of mind or predominant emotion: feeling; also the expression of mood especially in art or literature. Archaic: a fit of anger: rage; a prevailing attitude: disposition; a receptive state of mind predisposing to action; a distinctive atmosphere or context: aura.

In essence a *mood* is the way you feel emotionally or attitudinally at a particular point in time. One dictionary describes the word *moody* as an adjective that says: *if someone is moody, they are often unfriendly because they feel angry or unhappy.* Note that this definition of moody does not include *good moods.* Interestingly, in our society a happy person is never considered to be *moody* even though most people prefer good moods.

Clearly a mood is a temporary state of mind during which we are happy, sad, or angry and the prevailing emotion is coloring our view of the world. Moods originate in our experience. The events that occur in our lives make us feel a certain way and when the feeling is extreme or relentless it takes on the form of a mood. When we choose a mood, we choose to act out in way that is not usual to us.

Whether you like it or not, you really do choose your moods. When you get up in the morning, you are faced with a new day and a new opportunity to enjoy life. You can choose at the exact moment of waking to have a good or a bad day. That choice will then determine your mood. If you choose a good day, you will probably have a good day. However, it is possible that some intervening event may occur to cause your mood to sour during the course of the day. If you are resilient, you can deal with the challenge and resume your good day on a good note. On the other hand, if you choose to have a bad day, you will surely be successful. A day that starts off badly will support a bad mood throughout that day and perhaps for several more. If you want to get better at getting along with people try this: When you first awake each morning say out loud, *"I am going to have a great day today!"* Your husband or wife might think you have lost your mind, but that's okay. It will be worth it. Your mood will correspond with your attitude about the day to come and you will exude positive energy to everyone you come in contact with. That positive energy will be identified by others as a *good mood*. Nobody wants to hang out with someone in a bad mood, but people love to spend time with people who are in a good mood. We all carry an energy field or an aura about us that is perceptible to others. When those around us sense the positive energy of our good moods it gives them a feeling of wellbeing and warmth. That warmth will draw them to you and they will feel better for having spoken with you.

YOUR THOUGHTS ARE CONTROLLED BY YOU…AND YOU ALONE.

When you make a conscious effort to control your moods, you will in fact be sending a message to your brain that all is well. Your thoughts are controlled by you…and you alone. How you deal with any situation is your singular responsibility. If you find yourself feeling down and out, dig a little deeper and realize that you are still breathing and as long as you have life, you have hope. Stop the *woe is me* self talk; stop feeling sorry for yourself; and stop putting out negative vibrations to those you come into contact with. They have no control over your moods and they certainly do not deserve to have to suffer through your misery.

Do not blame someone else or an outside situation for your mood. If someone said something to make you angry and therefore put you into a bad mood, it was not them that created the bad mood…it was you. By choosing anger, you chose a bad mood. Anger is wasted energy and is seldom considered positive or helpful. However, it is unfortunately one of the most common and recurring emotions that human beings feel. A bad mood is often shrouded in anger. People don't want to even try to get along with an angry person in a foul mood and yet most of us spend at least some of our time in that state. The more evolved among us will recognize our folly and change our behavior to suit a given situation, or better yet, apologize to those we have inflicted ourselves upon. Many of us however, will not even be aware that our poor behavior is significant or is in any way unacceptable to others. When we fail to realize that we offend others with our moods, it is difficult to find people who want to get along with us.

Some bad moods are brought on by sadness or disappointment. When a person has experienced a death in their family, a sad mood is not only appropriate…it is healthy, for a short time. Human beings and some animals go through a mourning period which allows them to eventually accept the passing of one of their own. A well balanced person will generally bounce back after a few days or a few weeks at the most. If the mood continues on longer than that, they may require some professional counseling. When dealing with a person in a mood brought on by a tragic personal event, you should be kind and empathetic. Take the time to find out what their bad mood is all about. You wouldn't want to tell them to shape up and improve their attitude if their husband has just died or they are going through a sudden separation. If you find out that a bad mood is in fact due to a tragedy, you need to allow the person their space and a reasonable amount of grieving time.

OFTEN A PERSON WHO IS IN A BAD MOOD WILL CHOOSE COMPLAINING AS A SYMPTOM.

Unfortunately, a melancholy or sad mood is sometimes used as an attention-getter. The *poor me* attitude might be an attempt to right the wrongs that the person feels have been inflicted upon them. It can be a pitiful attempt to get attention and ultimately, the sympathy of people around them. Beware of someone who is constantly suffering from one problem after the next. Like the person who chooses to have a good day the minute he wakes up, these people have chosen sadness and disappointment as a lifestyle. For some reason buried deep in their psyche, they thrive on having everything go wrong. They travel from one tragedy to another in order to announce to the world that their life is worse than anyone else's and that they deserve the greatest amount of sympathy. Some of those sad folks will actually compete with others for the *worst life*. If someone suffers a tragic event, they will say something like, "Oh, you have no idea about tragedy. Let me tell you what happened to me!" These people deliberately go through life in a bad mood so that other folks will ask them what is wrong…then the flood gates open. The only way to get along with them is to buy into their negative energy and give them the sympathy they crave. That however, will create the transference of negative energy back to you, which will cause you to suffer right along with them. The best way to handle these people is to avoid them. When they don't get the sympathy they want, they will eventually tire of the game and leave you alone. If you are this person, understand that you are driving people away and that you would be much happier if you dropped the shroud of negativity.

Often a person who is in a bad mood will choose complaining as a symptom. They will find fault with others and lose patience with inanimate objects. You often hear of people swearing at other drivers on the road or smashing things that don't work. Even the most enlightened individuals have a crisis of patience from time to time, but some folks take it too far. If you know someone at work who is constantly finding something wrong with the company; your boss;

your co-workers, and/or the working conditions to the point that it becomes the identifying element of their persona, you probably have someone who is also often in a bad mood. They have chosen to be a vocal victim. They are pathologically *down* and they want to drag everyone down with them. This person might behave much the same way in their home life or they might have chosen work as the main target for their unhappiness. Probably because of something that happened during their formative years, they feel an inner inadequacy that transforms itself into unhappiness almost every time they begin to feel joy. They might also be trapped in a job they are fundamentally unsuited to and they are generating negativity to remove the focus from their poor performance or disengagement. They have committed to unhappiness and they will choose to be happy only when they can control the situation. Because of their feelings of inadequacy, they are naturally insecure. Controlling their expression of joyful emotion is the only real power they have. It is true that misery loves company so these people will generally spend a good deal of time trying to convince their co-workers of various conspiracies and warning them of fictitious, impending negative events. In the worst cases they will invent stories to harm those that do not buy into their negativity. Because they are so firmly attached to their negative energy many of these people will not respond to ordinary coaching and will spend their entire lives in a state of misery. They will reject any suggestion that their behavior is abhorrent and will see such accusations as just another threat to their already fractured ego. It is not easy to get along with these folks and it might be best for most of us not to try. Professional counseling might be the only answer as this moodiness is probably a symptom of a much deeper problem. If you choose to try to get along with an extremely negative person, ready yourself for disappointment and arm yourself with patience. You might want to consult with a professional coach or your employee assistance program for some help on how to approach the subject in order to begin improving the attitude of your unhappy friend.

Bad moods are also common in marriages. Husbands and wives sometimes use a bad mood as a method of communication. They will mope about or take on a gloomy look while only offering one word answers to the easiest of questions. Instead of saying, "Hey it was our anniversary yesterday and you forgot!" they might become silent and not say anything meaningful to their partner until he or she figures it out on their own.

Moods can be the result of fear in the moody person. They may be having trouble working up the courage to deal with a problem, so the mood is used as a tool to get someone to ask them what the problem is. Once that question is asked, the person is free to unload their problem onto the other person, thereby freeing their mind from the pain and allowing themselves the luxury of dealing with it.

A mood is often used as a way to say, "I am sad or angry and I am not going to tell you why. Instead I am going to make your life a living hell of silence." Isn't it interesting that people actually believe that they can get their point across by not communicating in any meaningful way other than facial expressions and body language? Behavior experts will tell you that fifty-five percent of human communication is non-verbal. However, you cannot tell someone exactly *what* is wrong if you don't use words. When you adopt a silent bad mood your intent is to cause emotional harm to another person or persons. You want them to suffer, just as you are suffering. Using a mood as a weapon is a great way to end a relationship completely even though that is seldom the intent of it. The mood is usually utilized to get some sort of attention but often it creates a back-fire effect instead. Stop moping around; stop the silent treatment; and get that frown off your face if you want to get along with people. It is quite simple: ***Bad moods are bad!***

HAPPINESS IS GOOD! DON'T KNOCK IT!

It would not be reasonable to leave a chapter on moods without talking about good moods. Don't you just hate those people who are in a good mood all the time? Why on earth are they so darned happy? Who cares? Happiness is good! Don't knock it! If you are in a good mood and someone questions your motives, don't listen to them. Have the courage to remain joyful in the face of misery. Your life and even your health will be better for it.

Unlike during a bad mood, non-verbal communication works very well during a good mood. A smile or a wink and a twinkle in the eye can bring joy to another person. When you are smiling or whistling joyfully, people will find you approachable. Your smile will indicate openness. Whistling or singing will indicate a carefree sense of abandon that drips of contentment. When you are in an obviously great mood, you will create opportunities for new friendships and positive, constructive communication because people are irresistibly drawn to you.

If you are friendly and smiley with people you buy things from, you will find that your good nature is returned. Once while changing planes on a lengthy cross country flight, I was forced to line up with a lot of other people to request an upgrade to better seating from an obviously harried and tired airline representative. I was in a good mood because I was looking forward to the trip. I was going to meet a good friend in Toronto and have dinner with him later that night and I was not in a hurry because I had lots of time to get there. When it was my turn to speak with her, I marched right up with a big smile on my face and said in a bright sing-songy voice, "Hi, how are you today?" she barely glanced at me while muttering something about how many people had come to her for an upgrade, how another connecting flight was late, and how the computer had a glitch which prevented her from knowing just how much preferred seating was available. Seeing her distress, I told her that this was a minor thing for me and because I could see that she had huge problems, I would be happy to sit in the seat that my travel agent had arranged for me. As I began to move away from the service desk, I said, "I hope things go better for you on the next flight."

I smiled at her again as I backed away. When she looked up and saw my toothy grin, she said, "Mr. Kehl, would you mind standing right over there while I try something?" I responded in the affirmative and stood a few feet away while the next ten people approached her. Most walked away with frowns and mumbles. Just when I thought I was going to have to sit in the nether regions of the plane, squished between a sumo wrestler and a chatty travelling salesman, she looked over my way and motioned me toward her. "You know something, Mr. Kehl your great attitude has paid off. I have you in row one in business class and I think you will be very happy with your seat! Thanks for your patience." Her smile was genuine and she almost had a look of gratitude on her face. When I got on the plane, I realized that not only was I in the front row, but I was the *only* passenger in the row. The seat next to me was empty for the entire flight. As I sipped my merlot and chomped away at my filet mignon while hurtling through the friendly skies, I noticed that very few of the folks who had asked for upgrades actually made it into the business class section at all. I attributed this bit of good fortune to the fact that I was in a good mood that day! It is very simple: ***Good moods are good!***

Your life will be enriched tremendously if you can always muster up a pleasant demeanor and a good attitude. When you are happy you will make others happy. Always give thought to your mood and how the manifestation of it may be affecting those around you. This simple technique will make getting along with people very easy.

What did we learn in Chapter Three?

• A mood is a temporary state of mind during which we are happy, sad or angry.

• Human Beings choose their moods.

• You can make a conscious choice to be in a good mood.

• Anger is wasted energy.

• A poor mood is appropriate after a tragic loss.

• Some people use moods to get attention.

• Some people like to bring others into their bad moods by complaining.

• People with chronic moodiness may require professional help.

• A moody person might use silence as a weapon.

• A good mood can create opportunities.

• People you deal with will treat you better when you are in a good mood.

• A constant good mood will enrich your life.

IS MONEY THE ROOT OF ALL EVIL?

"Money and status are good to have but they do not make you a better person."

CHAPTER 4

In North America, most people strive for status and wealth throughout their entire lives. The *American Dream* as it is known suggests that everyone in America is capable of being rich and important. We all come out of the womb with the potential for greatness. One human baby looks pretty much like the next and the intelligence and aptitude levels of each one are only slightly different than those of the next. DNA, surroundings, and life events will play a role in determining how well each will do. No matter what happens during our lives most of us go through it with the intense hope that somehow, someway we will acquire a lot of money someday. Discussions of, "What would you do if you won the lottery?" abound in lunchrooms and coffee shops all over North America. The dream of wealth is almost overwhelming for most folks and yet there is only room for a handful of people at the top. For very human reasons, that handful of people is resented and maligned by millions of others who are still striving to find the pot of gold at the end of the rainbow. Most people work hard all their lives only to end up with a small pension and a senior citizen discount at the movie theatre. Only a select few are able to acquire enough wealth to be considered rich by North American standards. Some are lucky enough to inherit a lot of money and others actually do have the great fortune to win a lottery. However, most people who end up with a huge amount of money have a marketable skill or talent and most work very hard to accumulate their wealth. The right combination of wealth-building talent and opportunity, like lightning, only strikes a few mortals over the course of a lifetime.

WE HAVE AN UNSPOKEN CLASS SYSTEM IN NORTH AMERICA…

In North America a person is considered wealthy when they have at least one million dollars of net assets. They are the fabled *millionaires*. There are various factors that can help you become a millionaire, but statistically a self-employed business owner is much more likely to become a millionaire than a person who works for someone else. People who own their own home also tend to accumulate more wealth than those who rent. It is a fact that on a national basis, those who do not graduate from high school accumulate a much smaller net worth during the course of their lives than those with college diplomas. It is important to note that in each one of these cases the disparity in wealth is dramatic and the gap continues to widen with each passing year. That disparity tends to cause a good deal of animosity amongst all of our citizens in all socio-economic classifications. We have an unspoken class system in North America which causes a good deal of social malaise.

Like most children, I went to school with a bunch of kids that were just like me. We lived in a neighborhood where the houses were all about the same size and we all wore blue jeans and running shoes. Our mothers and fathers were salesmen, secretaries, mill workers, plumbers and electricians. I was an average student like most of my friends and we all dreamed of being rich. We spent our recesses drooling over the lifestyles of the rich and famous and we loved to talk about someone's father who just bought something really expensive or whose parents were going on a trip to Hawaii. We all took the same courses and we all studied at approximately the same level. You might assume from the similarities in our lives, that we would all turn out the same and like our parents end up living in the same neighborhood, driving minivans. However, that is not the case. Some of my classmates have done extremely well on a wealth and status basis, and some have done extremely poorly. Interestingly many of the *popular* kids who had the world by the tail because of an outgoing personality or a great dunk shot in high school did not go on to great wealth and status at all. In fact most of them have hardly been seen or heard from since graduation. Many of the most intelligent kids who routinely brought home spectacular report cards faded away into mediocre anonymity once they left the hallowed halls of learning. Conversely, a lot of the mediocre kids found their talent and exerted their drive to its best benefit only after they left school.

I LEARNED FROM THE RICH KIDS THAT MONEY CAN BECOME AN EVIL FORCE.

We had a few rich kids in my school. They would not be considered rich by Donald Trump standards, but they did seem to live better and they wore better running shoes than the rest of us. They were often taken on exotic holidays and some of them had the luxury of a family summer home at a nearby lake. Motorcycles, boats, and the trappings of wealth filled their conversations. Their weekend adventures were ever so much more interesting than those of us who spent our time kicking a ball around at the park on our weekends. I learned from the rich kids that money can become an evil force. It seems to cause some people to become arrogant and aloof. It sometimes makes ordinary people with ordinary talent believe that they are somehow or other a more evolved life form than those people who have less of it. The sad part of it was that those of us who did not have a lot of money had no control over our lack of wealth. We were children after all. We lived with our parents and it was their lack of wealth that made us ordinary kids just as it was the wealth of the parents of the rich kids that made them rich kids. Even though these kids had never earned a penny in their lives, they seemed to feel that they had a right to take credit for the hard work and generosity of their parents.

Are you thinking what I am thinking right now? Here we go again… that old human chestnut of competition has reared its ugly head again. While the rich kids were lording their wealth over us, we were speaking badly of them…to their faces and behind their backs. It became great sport to pick on the rich kids in an attempt to make them feel badly about their wealth. Speaking badly of them behind their backs seemed to make us feel better about ourselves. Somehow we felt elevated by our indictments of their richness and alleged conceit. Our animosity was misplaced however, since it was their parents that were rich; not them. *"If they didn't brag so much, we wouldn't insult them so much,"* we thought. In reality, if we had been honest with ourselves we would have admitted that our bad attitude toward the rich kid was driven by envy. We wanted what they had and deep down in the cellars of our psyches we felt that it was unfair that they should have so much when we had so little. The rich kids bragged about their abundance because in their minds, having more stuff than the other kids was something to be proud of. It made them special but let us not forget this old adage: "*Pride Goethe before a fall.*" All of us kids were guilty of an immature lack of social awareness. We were also guilty of not getting along with people for totally invalid reasons. By the way, in the scenario I just described, the children, both rich and poor, were learning behavior that they would carry with them throughout their lives. Their feelings about money and wealthy people would not change when they became adults unless they made a conscious decision to think differently.

In some of the more affluent neighborhoods, where numerous rich kids are mixed with poor and middle class kids, money sometimes causes a class system to emerge. In those schools, the rich kids will become a social class unto themselves, creating an informal private club that only those of obvious wealth can join. Those of lesser wealth are to be excluded and only occasionally will a middle class child be allowed to hang out with the rich kids. When that happens it is often because the wealthier kids have an ulterior motive for allowing the lesser child in or the lesser child simply has an extraordinary ability to socialize with almost anyone. Any child who is able to run that gauntlet and actually cross the social barrier will probably be very successful in life.

Money creates tangible but less visible divides between adults as well. Adults will generally have learned some social skills and a much more advanced sense of social awareness by the time they become wealthy in their own right. The schoolyard name calling and backstabbing will usually be left behind at school. Nevertheless, some of the wealthy people I know have a knack for speaking about things that a middle class person simply cannot comprehend. Great discussions about multi-million dollar real estate deals and stock market transactions leave most people cold. However some of these wealthy guys don't seem to realize that their money conversations are at the very least boring, and at worst, maddening to the average person. The less-wealthy listener will have trouble understanding whether or not the wealthy folks are being boastful or if perhaps they actually think that their middle class conversation partner is in the same wealth category. Either way, a situation is being set up that will make the less-wealthy person uncomfortable. They will probably not want to admit that they cannot relate to the discussion because they cannot afford to purchase the things that the rich guys have, and they will not want to bring attention to their own lesser financial position.

If wealthy folks want to get along with average people, they need to understand that their money makes them a target for lack of trust from others. In North America there is an all too common feeling that wealth is identified by greed and avarice, and therefore the typical *millionaire* is not to be trusted. Just being in the presence of a millionaire is an unpleasant and discomforting event for some people. I prefer not to make the assumption that wealthy folks are bad in any way. I believe that most of them worked very hard to get where they are. When confronted by insensitive discussion from one of them, it is best to simply point out that you do not have the wealth that they do. Put them on notice that you cannot engage in conversations about fabulous real estate or stock deals and try to find some middle ground. Don't assume that millionaires don't want to talk to you either. They are just as anxious for companionship and healthy conversation about normal, everyday things as you are. The important thing to remember is that wealth does not make a person better than anyone else, nor does it make him or her any worse.

"NEITHER A BORROWER NOR A LENDER BE"

While we are on the subject of money, let's talk about lending. There is an old saying that goes: *"Neither a borrower nor a lender, be."* I agree with that. Lending money is one of the most dangerous things you can do when it comes to relationships. Every time I have lent money to someone, and it was not paid back at the date and time that we agreed upon, I was initially disappointed. As time passed, the disappointment turned to frustration and finally, frustration turned to anger. By the time I got the money back, I was generally so angry that my judgment was clouded to the point that I didn't even want the money back. I just wanted the borrower to suffer as much disappointment and frustration as I had. I did not like the fact that if I got the money back, they would be off the hook without further punishment from me. My outward reactions to such situations were animated angry talk or the age-old *silent treatment*. I assumed that a raised voice or non-verbal communication of frowns, crossed arms, and grunts would surely cause this person to think twice about messing with me again. In reality, all it did was cause them to think that I was an over-reactive jerk. Keep in mind that we are not talking about a lot of money here. In high school, I once held a grudge against a very nice young fellow for months because he did not repay me the two dollars that I had lent him for lunch. In later years, I lost my cool with a neighbor who had borrowed some surplus fencing lumber that I had lying beside my house. He did act irresponsibly in that it took him almost a year to repay me for the lumber, but frankly the rift caused irreversible damage to our relationship that I had not intended and did not want. Both of these scenarios are examples of people not getting along with people for very poor reasons. Both would have been easy to deal with in a cordial fashion or alternatively, both could have been overlooked with no harm to me or to the relationships. I chose to *make mountains out of molehills,* which is what people often do when money is involved.

Money naturally causes suspicion and loss of trust amongst everyone involved with it. The trust issue is probably most prevalent with husbands and wives because marriages have more mutual money dealings than any of the other normal human relationships. As we know, money is a leading cause of divorce and it is a constant source of annoyance and discomfort for both parties. Married folks need to sit down early in their union and talk about money in order to devise a plan for handling it that will not impact negatively on either of them. Once they have a mutually agreeable plan, they need to stick to it.

In the worst case scenarios people have been known to completely sever relationships with other people due to disputes over money. This happens to husbands and wives, fathers and sons, brothers and sisters, along with other relationships of all kinds. The initial intent is to make a point and bring attention to the wrong that the injured party feels but the actual and final effect may be dissolution of the relationship and an end to communication. While one party is making a point, the other party is rigidly and stubbornly refusing to admit that they have done anything wrong. The human competitive spirit and its accompanying drive to be *right* can be so overwhelming that people will sacrifice themselves to it. They will in effect, *throw themselves on their swords* and give up that which they love the most in order to make a point. It is hard to get along with people that you have eliminated from your life. Don't make that mistake. If things begin to escalate to that level, sit back and think about the situation. When bathed in the calm, cool light of reason, you will probably begin to feel that the issue is not so great that you cannot get over it. It is just money, after all. It is not *world peace* and it is not worth losing a relationship over.

When discussing money, I have to mention *greed*. Normal, sane human beings can be driven to some fairly abnormal and insane acts because of their desire for money. When thieves are born, they are just cute babies. They have no criminal tendencies. They know nothing of the world and certainly have no need for money. Unfortunately, while growing up, children gain an appreciation of money that occasionally verges on the pathological. In a negative environment, when they are old enough, some of them end up committing crimes in order to improve their financial positions. The crimes can be major or minor; ranging from embezzlement to armed robbery, but the intent is the same…they need to acquire money even if it means being caught and put in jail. Their greed has overtaken all of the other virtues they may have acquired during their lives. Those unfortunate folks who grow up to become criminals have lost their way and usually once they are caught, it is too late for them to find their way back. I accept that some folks are so destitute that thievery is a matter of survival and greed has little to do with it. Those people are usually the product of extremely negative environments where homelessness, drug addiction or alcoholism abounds. They have little or no chance to earn a normal living and theft is a way of life. The world needs to establish some better social programs for them, but that subject is better left to another book.

Even *normal,* upstanding folks who don't become criminals can exhibit symptoms of greed. Some will lie and cheat in order to acquire more money. Some force their will or their position on others to get their way and make more money. Some will betray friends and relatives in order to improve their financial position. They do not believe that their avarice is serious and they do not believe that they are really being dishonest. This is one of the tendencies of human beings that I find least attractive. It often starts at an early age with sneaky kids realizing that they can have whatever they want with just a little bit of trickery or some nasty bullying. If the culture they grow up in encourages that type of behavior, they will have trouble avoiding the tendency toward greedy behavior later in life. If you see your children acting this way, put a stop to it at an early age. It is neither cute nor funny and it may have life-changing implications in later years.

The title of this chapter asks: Is money the root of all evil? The answer is *NO!* The fact of the matter is that people are the root of all evil! Money is just an enabler that encourages people to create evil in their minds.

What did we learn in Chapter Four?

- Only a handful of people are destined to be rich and they are often resented by those not so fortunate.

- Rich people generally work very hard to accumulate wealth.

- Children learn to covet wealth during their formative years. Competition surrounding wealth begins at an early age.

- We have an unspoken class system in North America.

- Money can create unhealthy competition.

- Wealth may be accompanied by insensitivity and a lack of social awareness.

- Money is often at the centre of trust issues.

- Lending money can lead to relationship challenges. "Neither a borrower or a lender, be."

- Money can destroy relationships of all kinds.

- Greed begins at an early age and if left unchecked may become pathological.

- Money is not the root of all evil. People create evil in their minds!

I KNEW I WOULDN'T LIKE HIM THE MINUTE I LAID EYES ON HIM!

"We all have an aura about us that is the manifestation of the energy and essence of our soul."

CHAPTER 5

Have you ever disliked someone the minute you met him or her? Have you ever had someone ask you why you don't like someone, and found yourself stuck for an answer? At that moment, you may have tilted your head to one side and said, "I really don't know why I don't like her. She just gives me the creeps."

Occasionally, you might meet someone who is immensely popular with seemingly everyone you know but is totally repugnant to you. You might not be able to figure out why so many people like him and you might be wishing they would stop. In your mind, it is important that those around you feel the same way about him as you do. You might be frustrated by the adulation he receives from others and you might overtly snub him or drop sarcastic remarks about him every chance you get. If you develop a serious enough prejudice against him, you might begin to insult him directly and at the worst you might actually feel hatred for him.

Does any of this sound familiar? People have a tendency to launch covert, silent attacks against other people on a regular basis. For one reason or another, we can look at someone in passing or while being introduced to them only to find that we are almost immediately ill at ease. In other cases, we can look at someone or shake their hand and feel immediate warmth or an overwhelming desire to spend time with them, in order to get to know them better. Why do human beings have such contradictory behavior when in the presence of a variety of other human beings?

WHEN YOU ARE BORN YOU ARE IMMEDIATELY SWEPT INTO AN ALL-ENVELOPING OCEAN OF OTHER PEOPLE'S PREJUDICES.

Some of our feeling about other people comes from imprinting. When you are born, you are immediately swept into an all-enveloping ocean of other people's prejudices. As you age and your cognizance increases, you become a child of your environment. Your thoughts, perceptions, and prejudices are woven at least partially from the fabric of your family's cultural values. You might hear your mother speaking badly of a neighbor; you might see your father crossing his arms defiantly while listening to his paperboy's excuses for a newspaper that is delivered late; you will probably hear your siblings' fighting over who likes whom best. As the scene of your life unfolds, you become the unavoidable product of it. You may decide to like someone or something that your parents don't like but chances are, you will develop the same or similar likes and dislikes that they have no matter how hard you resist. Unfortunately, this is exactly what your parents want. They want you to dislike the same people they dislike and they want you to be afraid of people that they don't trust. They believe that their job is to make you into the **best** person they can in order to protect you and make you successful. In many cases, the person they want you to become looks, sounds, and **acts** just like them! You should only allow yourself to be exactly like your parents if you are certain they are the very best people in the world.

Often when you attempt to move away from family values, your family will attempt to drag you back in. If it becomes apparent that you are spending time with the son or daughter of someone your parents do not approve of, they might express displeasure with your choice of friends. At the very least, they will say nothing positive about your friend that might indicate approval. Their deafening silence will be your clue that they do not approve. At worst, they will be overtly critical and perhaps even tell you not to associate with that person. The same can happen with a sister or brother who does not want you to associate with the siblings of someone he or she does not get along with. These scenarios have been going on all over the world, every day of every year, since the world began.

When your family and friends tell you that this person or that person, or perhaps an entire race or culture is bad, you quite naturally remember it. You may fight the feeling and if you are of strong character you might even overcome it. Most of us though, will harbor some doubt, fear or outright prejudice for many years to come. Again, that is what those close to us desire. When you don't react in the way they want, they will resort to negativity. Negative reinforcement is a popular way to force others to our own way of thinking. In the case of a sibling for example, when your brother tells you that someone should not be your friend and you reject the notion, he might counter with a series of attacks on that person in order to enforce his point of view. The attacks could be in the form of racial slurs, personal insults, or any number of fabricated stories that will put doubt in your mind. If he is convincing enough, you might begin to believe not only that your potential friend has serious shortcomings, but also that everyone *like* him carries the same negative genes. If you succumb to this negative pressure you will lay the groundwork for a lifetime of prejudice that will bring pain to others and a harmful loss of credibility to you each time you exercise it.

Life is so much lighter and easy to live without prejudice. Despite that, the old adage, *"live and let live"* seems to be reserved for saints and angels. I have not met many people in my life who truly live those words.

Often when you dislike someone *on-sight* your feeling of uneasiness is based in fear. For example, comedians often make jokes about people who are afraid of clowns. Hollywood has even made movies about horrible scary, clowns. I am not a fan of clowns myself. My feelings for them have nothing to do with movies or comedians, however. At the tender age of six years old, I was introduced to a clown at the Pacific National Exhibition in Vancouver. He was a very tall man with massive shoes; a polka dotted pajama-like outfit, and a wig of some curly red stuff that almost resembled human hair. Along with that he had painted on some of the most grotesquely colorful makeup I have ever seen. He had a huge grin painted on his face, but it was obvious to me that his real lips were not curved in the shape of a normal human smile at all. I recall that he was extremely scary looking at the time but I realize now that his intention was to look funny.

I was wandering through the fair with my parents and my brother on that sunny summer day when the clown approached me. He fixed his gaze on my face and walked straight toward me with his hand outstretched in what I took as intent to harm me in some way. The only things about this man that I recognized as normal and human were his eyes. The rest of his visage was disfigured, improperly colored, and overtly hideous. When I looked into his eyes, I did not like what I saw. All I could see were two black holes with no warmth and no indication of joy or even good humor. As he reached out to me, I looked up at my mother. Seeing the fear in my eyes, she said, *"Go ahead, Wayne. It's okay. He's just a clown!"* I reached my hand out and the huge, white-gloved paw of the mysterious, sullen stranger immediately grabbed it and began pumping my arm up and down furiously. I did not like the fact that he had me firmly by the hand and despite the fact that my family was surrounding me, I was feeling extreme anxiety and an overwhelming need to escape his grip. I squirmed about and finally gave a hard tug, pulling my little hand out of his huge mitt. When I had fully liberated myself and backed away, he said nothing. He merely peered at me with a look that I took for disgust, (it was hard to tell what he was thinking under all of the makeup), shrugged his shoulders, and wandered off to bring joy into the life of some other unsuspecting child. My heart had been beating wildly throughout this, my first clown-encounter and seeing him moving slowly but deliberately away from me brought relief and a renewed feeling of wellbeing. Not only had I encountered the scary beast; I had survived the experience! Of course when I told this story to my friends at school the following Monday, I bragged about how I had met a clown at the Pacific National Exhibition and shook his hand. I made it sound like one of the best experiences of my life to date. However, as I write this, I have come to the disturbing realization that even though it happened fifty years ago, I have never forgotten it. By the way: I have never shaken hands with a clown since. My prejudice toward clowns was based in a fear that I don't really understand, but it was very real and it clouded my judgment. Perhaps now that I have faced my fear and had the courage to publish it for the world to read, I will be able to put it aside and become a fan of those mysterious clown creatures.

The reason my clown story appears here is to point out how the human mind works. We don't trust what we don't understand and we push away from people we don't trust. If the lack of trust is dramatic enough, it sometimes manifests itself as fear. In a very short time, lack of trust, coupled with fear can turn into dislike and dislike can turn into hatred, under the right circumstances.

I have been the victim of human distrust myself. Early in my career as an insurance agent I realized that a lot of people do not enjoy purchasing home and automobile insurance and subsequently do not trust the people who sell it. Without getting into a long and boring dissertation about insurance, I think it safe to say that general insurance is one of the most universally misunderstood products available on our planet. Insurance simply does not cover *every* situation and most people who suffer an uninsured loss feel deserted and even cheated by their insurance company. The emotion that arises after an uninsured claim, often leads to anger and distrust. As a purveyor of the product for over thirty years, I have occasionally felt the burning brunt of those negative emotions. In one case, I sat through a very uncomfortable dinner with a friend who had brought one of his clients along to meet me. Unbeknownst to him my friend's client had recently suffered an uninsured claim on his automobile and some years prior had been paid less than he felt he deserved after a theft at his jobsite. When the unhappy insurance buyer was introduced to me, he was very charming and very friendly. At that point he had no idea of my occupation. The three of us carried on a very pleasant chat about the weather and recent political happenings for some time, and then just when I thought I was in for a very enjoyable evening, he asked me what I did for a living. When I answered that I was an insurance agent, his body stiffened and his demeanor changed dramatically. He turned away from me and began speaking with my friend as though I no longer existed. As uncomfortable as this was, I forged on attempting to involve myself in the conversation. Finally, when I thought that any hope of my being part of the discussion was lost, the man turned to me and said, *"I hate insurance!"* Those words were not foreign to me, as I had heard them many times before.

"Really? Why do you hate insurance so much?" I asked.

"Because every time I try to make a claim on it, I get screwed!" he retorted as he stared defiantly into my eyes, silently daring me to take on the challenge to convince him otherwise. I took the challenge and spent the next three hours explaining, not only the reasons why his claims had been problematic, but also how he could go about protecting himself in the future. I also came up with a plan to better handle his insurance portfolio. Because I have always been a big believer in the value of insurance, I spoke honestly from my heart and he could sense that I was sincere. He even admitted to me that he felt that I genuinely wanted to help him. Before the evening was over, he had decided to move all of his insurance to my agency and he apologized for thinking

badly of me. The final victory for me was when he said, *"I like you. You're not a bad guy!"*

WHEN YOU ARE ANGRY, YOUR AURA WILL QUITE NATURALLY PUSH PEOPLE AWAY.

What I experienced was the wrath of a man who had been disappointed by the insurance industry and believed that all people involved in it must be bad. He sensed from the attitudes and actions of the people that he dealt with on insurance in the past that all insurance people are inherently evil. However, when I showed genuine concern and a good deal of empathy for his problems, his view of me changed. In essence then, because of my positive response to his obvious pain, he felt that my aura was more appealing than the auras of the other insurance people he had come in contact with in the past. What many people refer to, as our *aura,* is the manifestation of the energy and essence of our soul. Some writers and new-age philosophers will tell you that you can actually see the aura around someone. I do not buy into that theory, but I do believe that we all carry an energy field around us that emits feelings that are palpable to those we come into contact with. Our aura is not any particular color and it does not snap and crackle with electrical energy. It does however force others to feel a certain way about us. The way others feel about us at any period of time is a direct response to the positive or negative energy that we are pushing into our aura. If you are feeling depressed, your aura will indicate that you are down. Your energy field will be cold. At that point, people around you will know that you need to be treated differently than if you were to win a lottery. In that event, your aura will be very warm and people will know that you will happily accept warmth, joy and humor from them. When you are angry, your aura will quite naturally push people away. Your angry aura will be warmer than your happy aura but it will contain negative heat that will cause fear or revulsion in others. Your depressed aura is cold, but it will not create fear in others. It will, in fact often cause others to attempt to give some of their own warmth to you so that you may return to your normally positive aura. Auras are not always directly related to moods however. Sometimes they have more to do with attitude.

At this point, I have to return to a brief discussion on the competitiveness of human beings. Most of us wish to believe that we are very good at *something*. It may be that we think we are smart, good looking, funny or perhaps on a larger scale we believe we are great managers, public speakers or salesmen. When we come into contact with other people with attributes similar to our own, our auras may clash. For example, if you believe that you are the best salesman in your office and find out that a new *hotshot* has been hired, you will feel threatened and your aura will cool off in the presence of his warm optimistic aura. If that happens, your initial meeting with him will be uncomfortable and stilted. You will have trouble thinking of anything to talk about and afterwards, you might say to an ally, "I knew I wouldn't like him the minute I laid eyes on him!" Alternatively, you could overcome your fear of being upstaged by this interloper and deliberately adopt a positive attitude that will manifest itself as a warm aura that will attract him to you. That attitude of course will make it much easier for you both to get along with each other. I have seen a negative aura occur due to competitiveness surrounding things as simple as height, weight, and sense of humor. I have also seen it occur when *big-ticket* items like management ability, work ethic, and the love between two people are involved. In those situations, the fear of losing the power of one's own personal attributes, ability, or stature causes cold auras to appear, and bad relationships to result. This phenomenon is really not due to some people having a supernatural ability to sense evil or malicious intent in the auras of others as they might think. It is instead a product of simple envy, jealousy, or fear of failure.

THERE ARE PEOPLE IN THE WORLD WHO ARE IN FACT, EVIL!

In some cases, you might immediately dislike someone for very a good reason. There are people in the world who are in fact, evil! They are thieves, rapists, child molesters, murderers and the like. Unless they are completely insane and totally unaware of where they are or who they are, they fully understand and accept that they are inherently bad. Even the vilest of criminals knows he or she is bad. Criminals grow up on planet earth like the rest of us and are aware of society's standards. They know that breaking into people's homes or killing their neighbors is not acceptable anywhere in the world. They live with guilt and they know that if they are caught they will be incarcerated or at worst, executed. They live with evil and fear in their hearts twenty-four hours of every day. It might be possible to rehabilitate some of these people, but until that happens, they are by definition...*evil!* What kind of aura would you expect to find around one of these people?

People with criminal backgrounds and those who live with criminal intent in their hearts put off cold and frightening auras. If you meet one of these people, you will sense that *something* is wrong. You won't be able to define exactly what it is about the person before you, but you will feel a sense of uneasiness. After the person is gone, you might say, *"That guy really made me uncomfortable."* The reason for your discomfort is the fact that an evil person, feeling his or her own evil will unavoidably emit an aura of negativity. Even con artists, who are adept at faking social awareness in order to dupe their victims, have an internal evilness about them that will be felt by others. As you are being taken advantage of by one of these guys, you might be feeling that there is just *something* about him that you don't like. Pay attention to that feeling. If you really don't like someone the minute you lay eyes on him, and there are no influencing factors such as jealousy, imprinting or prior experience, there is a possibility that they have an evil heart and intend to take advantage of you or harm you in some way.

YOU MUST GIVE EVERY PERSON A FAIR CHANCE TO BECOME A POSITIVE FORCE IN YOUR LIFE.

Be careful that you are not simply influenced by the appearance of people. Often when someone repels us it is because of a physical appearance or manner of dress that reminds us of another person that we have had bad experiences with in the past. We are sometimes influenced negatively by a radical or unusual appearance as well. Folks with politically incorrect dreadlocks or multiple body piercings were cute little babies when they were borne and with luck and good fortune, they will be kindly, happy senior citizens before they die. They simply chose a different appearance than yours at the moment in time when you met them. Don't worry…hair and jewelry on someone else's body cannot hurt you! You must look beyond the outward physical appearance and focus on the aura of each person you meet. Get to know all human beings as individuals and make your relationship choices based on how you truly feel about the souls and auras of them after you have spent some time delving into their psyches.

You must give every person a fair chance to become a positive force in your life. It is important that you avoid negativity and endeavor to get to know everything you can about each person you meet. Only then will you find that getting along with people is easy.

What did we learn in Chapter Five?

- We often dislike people because of prejudice created by family influence and imprinting. Prejudice must be eliminated from your life.

- Distrust can lead to dislike which can lead to hate.

- A positive attitude can turn enemies into friends.

- We all create an aura for ourselves. Choose a good attitude and a good mood and you will create a good aura.

- We sometimes dislike people because we feel they are competing with us for our personal power base.

- A negative energy field surrounds truly bad people.

- Don't judge a book by its cover. Personal appearance is not an indication of worthiness.

- Give every person a chance to become a positive force in your life.

DOES MY SPOUSE REALLY HATE ME, OR IS IT SOMETHING I SAID?

"A perfect marriage is a lifetime of agreements and disagreements, punctuated by occasional periods of pure joy."

CHAPTER 6

Marriage is the union of two people for an unspecified period of time that was once described as, *until death do us part.* However, in these modern times, with a North American divorce rate that is verging on sixty percent, it appears that death is no longer a necessary requirement or even a consideration prior to parting with the one's spouse. The promise to have and to hold is no longer time-bounded. In fact, marriage seems to have become a temporary, transitive thing that folks do for the sake of wedding gifts and a party rather than as an opportunity to share the joy of living with each other for a lifetime. Despite the alarming divorce rate, I believe that most people initially enter the bonds of marriage with a true and honest intention to stay married until one of them actually dies. If I am correct, why do so few of them get it right?

VERY FEW ANIMALS OTHER THAN MAN ACTUALLY MATE FOR LIFE.

The fact of the matter is that marriage…the permanent monogamous mating of two warm-blooded mammals, is not an expected or logical course of events in nature. Very few animals other than man actually mate for life. It is thought that beavers and bats do, but gorillas and chimpanzees, which are closer to man on the evolutionary chain, do not. Men are sexual creatures, permanently in heat and always ready to rut. Females of the human race too, are quite ready, willing, and able to have sexual encounters even during times when they are not technically *in heat*. Given the propensity and opportunity for human sexual encounters, it is surprising that anyone in the human race, male or female, has any desire to be married at all. Without the constraints of the marriage vows men and women could have exciting sexual encounters with a variety of partners every day of the week. Of course the various religions of the world and civilized society have determined that man cleaving to woman is the natural and appropriate thing to do. Billions of people all over the world have chosen marriage as a lifestyle for the past many centuries. Now we are finding that men and women in ever-increasing numbers are deciding that the political correctness of church and state-sanctioned marriage is not such a good thing in the long run. When they divorce, they are *doing what comes naturally,* joining the majority of the warm-blooded animals on our planet in the hedonistic candy store of life.

It is a fact that marriages lasted longer in the past. There were good and functional reasons for that. Early in the twentieth century a large portion of our population relied on farming for survival. Large families with a matriarch and patriarch firmly in control made sense. Large families were necessary because farms needed cheap labor to survive. The mother was needed to run the household and make the meals while the father acted as the manager and foreman to the children as they worked the fields and milked the cows. Divorce would simply not have worked in that environment. The delineation of male and female jobs was so precise that men seldom if ever, cooked food and women were generally not expected to operate machinery. If either spouse left the farm, it would surely fail and the family would starve. The same held true in a variety of family run businesses where the workload was shared and the company was to be passed on to successive generations of the clan. Finances dictated that divorce was not an option.

DIVORCED MEN WERE CONSIDERED POLITICALLY INCORRECT AND EVEN UNSTABLE.

In those days it was truly a man's world. Women were considered to be *in-home* support units. They were not deemed to be capable of working in male dominated professions and because of their biological cycles and feminine softness, were treated as second-class citizens. They were never paid as much as men despite their abilities, expertise or work ethic. They could only do *women's jobs,* which were generally menial and demeaning. If a woman did become divorced, she would be cast out of *proper* society and treated almost like someone with a communicable, deadly disease. Men ruled the world and along with their men's clubs and secret societies, they had a good number of affairs with loose women, divorced women and prostitutes. Even though men of the early twentieth century were able to practice their atavistic tendencies to mate outside of marriage, they generally remained with their wives just as their wives willingly stayed with them. In those times, divorced men too, were considered lower on society's scale than their married counterparts, since when a man had a wife by his side he presented the image that church and state wanted to see. Divorced men were considered politically incorrect and even unstable. In the nineteen-forties and fifties a divorce could actually prevent a man from attaining a promotion or pay raise at his place of employment. Men and women were tied together by marriage whether they liked it or not. Children were casualties of the shame of divorce as well since most kids were fortunate enough to grow up in what have been dubbed *nuclear families*...essentially, families with two parents. To be the product of a broken family was to be an oddity. Single-parent kids were pitied or ridiculed in the schoolyard and divorce was something that no one liked to talk out loud about. On an ironically positive note it seems that in this century, kids from nuclear families are the oddities and divorce is the norm. There is no longer the same stigma attached to being the child of a broken marriage.

In the nineteen-sixties and seventies, the world began to change, thanks to something called *women's liberation* or simply *women's lib*. A variety of very strong women, too numerous to mention, pioneered a movement to allow women to take their rightful place in society. Slowly but surely, women began to move out of the confines of their kitchens and their menial female occupations. They began to demand equal pay for equal work and they forced employers to provide time off for maternity in order to allow work and family life to intermingle. As I write this, I am aware that women have not gained complete equality with men in North American business, but they are light years ahead of where they were a century ago. That progress brought with it a sense of independence and a realization that women are no longer chained to the stoves that their male husbands bought for them. They too, can drive their own automobiles and buy their own houses. In the twenty-first century, women can do almost anything that men can...and they know it! Rightly or wrongly, depending on your perspective, financial independence has given women the courage to forsake their marriage vows. Divorce is no longer considered to be a violation of society's rules. It is in fact, the natural course of events for the majority of marriages in North America. Men have become liberated as well since a functional marriage is no longer a career requirement. Divorce is worn almost as a badge of honor by many of our more successful males. Marriage has fallen so far out of favor that many couples in the new millennium now make the conscious decision to live together without the bonds of marriage. That form of relationship is often referred to as *"common-law."* Couples who live in common-law marriages seem to believe that even though they have all of the responsibilities and appearances of married couples, the relationships are less confining because the unions have not been blessed by church or state. The lack of marriage licenses and vows makes separation emotionally and psychologically more palatable. It is almost as if many couples assume that their relationships will not last anyway, so the fewer barriers to freedom there are, the better.

As much as I accept that divorce is a common, acceptable life choice in the new millennium, I have observed that it causes a good deal of unnecessary stress and emotional turmoil for its participants. I have also observed that even after divorce, a large number of couples continue to stay in touch and many of them consider themselves good friends long after parting. I find it perplexing that people who consider themselves friends, have made the effort to get married, and in many cases, have had children together, can so easily make the conscious decision to divorce. This all too common phenomenon is in stark contrast to many of the marriages of the prior millennium when people stayed together in holy wedlock even after they had learned to hate each other.

To understand why married people do not get along we simply need to understand what drives romance, since romance is what drives most people to the vows of marriage. Love…that most compelling of emotions, forces people to make the decision to get married in the first place. For love to exist, there must be attraction, trust, respect, common interests and a meeting of the minds. Love can exist without sex for a time, but at some point sex too, becomes an essential element in every romantic relationship. When any one of the essential elements of love is shaken, the marriage begins to teeter, like a table with one broken leg. You can still use the table but it is quite annoying when it rocks back and forth. When two or more of the elements are eliminated, the union is likely to be terminated by one or both of the parties to it just as a two-legged table will not stand on its own.

As described earlier, love is often shaken by money, because when money becomes an issue between married partners, trust disappears. When trust disappears, respect goes with it. When trust and respect are gone, spouses often stop finding each other attractive. They may still acknowledge that the other person is aesthetically pleasing, but they are no longer attracted to them as a person. When they are no longer attracted, sex will usually stop occurring spontaneously and all of the elements of love that were once present may be replaced with resentment and in some cases, hatred.

REMAIN SINGLE UNTIL YOU ARE READY TO COMMIT FULLY.

Another sure way to end a marriage is to show potential romantic interest in another person. People who make the conscious decision to wed do not want to share their partner with other suitors. They want an exclusive relationship where all of the romantic and sexual interests of their partner are focused upon them. Unfortunately, temptations abound in today's divorce-laden society, and the public media is obsessed with sexuality. Men and women feel the need to be sexually attractive at all times as promoted by the clothing, cosmetics, and beer companies. It is much easier now for men and women to seek out or stumble across an additional love interest. When that occurs, another leg will be broken out from under the marriage-table and the vicious cycle of lost trust, lost respect, and lost love will begin again. If you want to get along with your spouse, keep your hands off of the people you meet and avoid the temptation to involve yourself with them. Don't even joke about romantic relationships with other people and do not use the excuse that you are just being friendly. Infidelity will end your marriage as surely as love drove you to the altar. If you want to stay married and enjoy a balanced lifestyle, remember that a brief *fling* could cause permanent pain. If you think that you will have trouble honoring your marriage vows, you probably won't disappoint yourself. If you feel that way, don't get married at all. Remain single until you are ready to commit fully. That way, you will prevent yourself and at least one other person from suffering the pain and strain of a broken marriage.

Many married people who don't have money or fidelity problems simply do not get along. That is because they do not have a meeting of the minds and generally have very few common interests. They are so removed from each other perceptually that they view the world from completely separate vantage points. One spouse might want to travel, while the other is afraid of flying. One might like steak while the other prefers salad. One might like camping and fishing while the other would rather stay home and read. Some spouses love to socialize while others prefer to be alone. If you want to have a happy marriage you really need to sort those things out prior to making the commitment to wed. When two people are attracted to each other, they will do a mating dance that sometimes includes non-deliberate deception. They will be so intent on pleasing the object of their affections that they will pretend to like what the other person likes, even to their own detriment. In some cases, the deception will be so complete that they will convince themselves that they suddenly like something that they have never liked before. Unfortunately as the years pass and they grow weary of the mating dance, they will pull away from the interests of their spouse and the marriage-table will begin to rock. Dig deep to find out what your love-interest really likes before you commit. Many people believe that they can *change* another person to fit the mold they have for them. They are deluding themselves. People simply cannot change completely. The underlying motivation of their needs and the direction of their natural behavior will always lead them back to the way they were before someone tried to change them. For example, if your future spouse is a hard drinking, foul-mouthed, philanderer when you meet him, he will not change because you want him to. It is more likely that he will want you to change to be more like him and he will encourage you to accept his unacceptable ways. He might fake it for a while, but he will not become the person you want him to be, no matter how hard you try. If you marry someone against your own better judgment because you feel a misdirected tug of superficial love, you will surely end up divorced or trapped in a loveless relationship.

I have also observed a lot of personal competition in marriages. There seems to be an overwhelming *need to be right* between married couples. The thing that many husbands and wives seem not to understand is that if they have divergent views or wants, they cannot satisfy both. If you have divergent views, negotiation and capitulation will have to occur. If one partner wants a new house and the other one doesn't, they cannot possibly both get what they want...unless they get divorced. And yet, couples will argue to the point of separation over issues that are much less important or expensive than real estate. They will both fight to get their own way until the only logical resolution is separation and/or divorce. If you want to get along with your spouse for a lifetime, you will have to get used to the concepts of negotiation, and capitulation. In some marriages, the couples will do a series of trades to keep their competition balanced and allow both to win an equal number of times. For example she might allow him to get a new boat, if she can go to New York on a shopping trip. That type of negotiation can become quite expensive but amazingly, it keeps a lot of marriages together for a very long time. The competitive need to win is prevalent in virtually every human relationship and marriage is no exception. You must understand that and be willing to deal with it before you make the decision to walk down the isle. If you expect to win every difference of opinion, you will be sadly disappointed and probably divorced in no time at all. At the very least, you will be miserable. Getting along with your spouse is easier if you let them have their way from time to time.

"PLEASE DON'T EMBARRASS ME TONIGHT!"

Competition in marriage rears its ugly head in the social arena as well. Women and men tend to expect their spouses to *act* a certain way in public. She might want him to wear a dark suit when she takes him to her staff Christmas party and he might expect her to wear a new dress when she goes to his. The way they dress is seldom of any interest to anyone at the party other than the two spouses, but if they do not agree, it will cause endless strife between them. Often a husband or wife will want his or her spouse to change the way they speak when in the presence of friends, colleagues, clients, or superiors. They will want him or her to be politically correct and say the right things in order to avoid any chance of embarrassment. Again, most of the people who will hear one or the other of the spouses will not care much about what is said during any of the conversations that they might have. Nevertheless, we often hear spouses saying to other spouses, "Please don't embarrass me tonight!" The only time one spouse would deliberately embarrass another spouse is when the marriage is near its end so don't worry about it. Most people will accept your spouse exactly as he or she is. Since other people are not involved in your personal marriage competition, they assume that your spouse is exactly what you want him or her to be and will be supportive of your relationship.

Let's talk about the kids. The children of divorced parents suffer the most and yet they are often part and parcel of the division. Due to the competitive nature of people, we often find that parents will vie for the affections of their mutual offspring. Dad will want to take them to a ball game, while mom will want them to play the piano. Dad will want to spend money for new toys, while mom will want to save for their education. Both want to do great things for their kids but often their actions have more to do with their own egos than the needs of the children. While mom and dad are arguing about what is best for the children, they are becoming less attracted to each other as life mates and the children know it. While you are battling, your children are listening and becoming more and more concerned that they are the reason for your fighting. If you want to get along with your spouse, you must agree on what the needs of the children really are. What the *best* child rearing methodology is has been debated and written about for decades. Dr. Spock and others have made a science of it, so I will not attempt to rewrite those books. However, it is important to understand that spouses must have a common point of view and must present a united front when dealing with their children. Even if your approach is unorthodox, both spouses should support it. Children who grow up in homes rife with parental discord tend to retaliate by displaying anti-social behavior outside of the home. *Troubled children* as they are known, are often troubled because their parents inadvertently trained them to be that way during their arguments. Even if your fights are not about the kids, have them in private where curious, little ears cannot hear you. Any discord is bad discord for children. If you are a parent, put your ego aside and make your children your sole focus for the eighteen or twenty years that they will be with you. The time you have with your children represents only about twenty five percent of your total lifetime, so why not make the best of it. You have one shot at it with each child, so try to get it right the first time. Your kids will be better for it and the bonus is that you will find it much easier to get along with your spouse. While they are under your roof, always think, *"kids-first!"* The damage that divorced couples do to themselves is not nearly as devastating or long lasting as the damage they do to their children.

Oh, and by the way…if you do get into an argument or disagreement, always limit your discussion to *one* item. Deal only with the situation at hand and resist the temptation to dredge up a bunch of other annoying things that have long since passed by. If you utilize old problems to win current arguments, you will drive the knife deeper and lose any chance you might have had to come to a mutually acceptable conclusion. When you bring up other negative situations, your partner will feel attacked and will quite naturally go on the defensive. He will stop being rational and will turn the tables, going on the attack against you. At that point the discussion is over and the war is on. Always remember... only dispute one thing at a time!

Finally, you need to sort out where you want to be in life before you select a spouse. Unfortunately, North American society has created various levels of financial success and notoriety that everyone in North America must fit into. Most folks proudly exist as a part of the hard-working middle class, while others feel the need to fly into the upper echelons of the rich and famous. Some folks are desperately poor through no fault of their own while some are fabulously rich due to good fortune or inheritance. Some folks want to rub shoulders with movie stars and politicians while others want to be anonymous and live in solitude. When you are selecting a spouse for life, you must move beyond the immediate physical attraction and loving *tug* that you feel and consider whether or not the object of your affections wants the same things that you do. If you are racing to the top of your political, entertainment, or business career while your spouse is trying desperately to hold you back, problems are bound to occur. Divorce is commonplace in marriages where one spouse is aggressive and successful while the other is reticent and insecure. Unless both spouses are completely supportive of each other and take pride in each other's accomplishments, the foundation of the marriage is on shaky ground. Put your emotional love on the back burner while you think seriously about your overall compatibility. Once you are certain that you are both headed in the same direction, it may be appropriate to think about marriage.

In deference to all of the songwriters and poets of the world I must say that *love is not always the answer*. Love is the starting point, but without common interests, common goals, and a meeting of the minds, a marriage will not succeed for a lifetime. On the positive side, when married people are truly in love and have learned the secrets of living in harmony, there is nothing better on earth. Good relationships are what make human beings the dominant creatures on our planet. It is not easy to have a great marriage, but it is worth the effort!

What did we learn in Chapter Six?

- Mating for life is not natural to human beings.

- Divorce was once considered to be politically incorrect but is quite acceptable now.

- A successful marriage must have a solid base of attraction, trust, respect, common interests and a meeting of the minds.

- People should be fully committed to a lifetime of marriage to one person before they wed.

- Fidelity between two marriage partners must be complete and pure for a marriage to last.

- Do not expect your spouse to *change.* Select a spouse that is already what you want.

- Take the competition out of your marriage if you want it to survive.

- If you must argue, only argue about one thing at a time.

- Think of your kids first. Your negative actions can destroy their lives.

- Make sure your spouse wants the same life that you do before you marry.

- Love is not the only answer to a good marriage.

CHAPTER SEVEN

IT'S JUST WORK, PEOPLE!

"Your job is not your life…It is just the place you go to make the money that funds your life"

CHAPTER 7

I have a friend in the personal development business who often says in a loud voice during his presentations, ***"It's just work, People!"*** I wish everyone on earth would adopt that way of thinking. Of course, he is referring to the stress, strain, depression, anger, and fear that so many workers feel because of their jobs. These problems exist all over North America and workers at all levels suffer from them everyday. Many people take their jobs so seriously that they actually suffer physical symptoms brought on by psychological stress because of their work activities. Work related anxiety attacks; fainting spells, and debilitating hypertension can overcome even the strongest of people. A lot of the problems people have at work stem from relationships with co-workers. One of the managers I worked for years ago used to joke about his insurance agency; *"This would be a great business, if it weren't for the people!"* He was of course joking about his staff and his clients, but I suspect there was a kernel of reality behind the humor.

HAVING AN OBSESSION WITH ONE'S WORK IS NEITHER A HEALTHY OR PRODUCTIVE USE OF TIME!

In North America, work life usually represents one third of any person's day for five days of most weeks. However, for some people it becomes the focus of their attention for two thirds of their time and some even have nightmares about it. For those with nightmares, work-focus takes up almost one hundred percent of their time. Having an obsession with one's work is neither a healthy or productive use of time. Bringing your job home with you is a sure way to annoy or bore your family and friends and it will eventually drive a wedge between you and your employer. Ultimately, you will resent your boss and your Company for making you feel the way you do. You will probably blame them for forcing you to do more work and carry more anxiety than necessary when in fact it is you who chooses obsession and anxiety. Look around at your co-workers. You will probably find that there are a good number of people in your department who are perfectly fine with their jobs and their workloads. You might resent them too, but remember that they are doing work very much like yours and yet they seem not to feel the same anxiety and stress that you do. Why is that? It is because they view their work differently than you do and they are able to accept their job as *just a job*. Some of them may even love doing the work that brings you so much unhappiness. Before you find fault with your Company, your boss, or your co-workers, look deeply into yourself. Are you in the right job? Perhaps not…maybe you should reconsider your choice of employment and set yourself free to spend one third of your life doing work that actually makes you smile. Remember this: ***"Successful people get to do work they enjoy everyday."*** If you are not suited to your work and do not enjoy it, you will not be successful and you will make those around you miserable while you are wasting their valuable time complaining about it. You won't find getting along with people easy at all if you are constantly complaining about work. While you are attempting to drag them into your world of negativity, your cold, negative aura will be driving them away.

I have also found that people who are not happy in their work sometimes turn out poor quality and bad service. They seem to feel that their customers should share in their misery, or that they are offering a mute protest to their employer through bad customer service. By sending out products that will not work properly or by being rude to customers, they feel that they are punishing their employer for their misery. Some of them are just so darned miserable that they are unaware of their own bad behavior or have passed the point of caring. At that point, it is important that *someone* do *something* to get to the root of the problem. Either the employer needs to employ some positive discipline and personal coaching, or the employee needs to admit that they have a problem. It is not fair or reasonable to expect paying customers to suffer due to workplace malaise.

Often the main source of anxiety at work is the people who work there. It is quite easy to be dragged down by a co-worker who is unhappy. The most dedicated toxic employees will actually spend their days and nights dreaming up reasons why they, along with everyone else should be unhappy at work. The old expression, *"misery loves company"* is more evident at work than anywhere else. Human beings deliberately live and work beside other human beings because fundamentally, just like wolves and other pack animals, they need a societal structure in order to survive. So that they may live comfortably in society, wolves and people need to form relationships with allies for safety, security, and nurturing. That being the case, people who are unhappy at work need allies who are also unhappy at work. If you let your guard down, and listen to the negativity of those people, you may inadvertently become one of their allies. The toxic employees will work hard to give you good and reasonable reasons to lose faith in your company, your boss, and some of your other co-workers. Negativity breeds negativity and nothing good ever comes from it. It is a self-fulfilling prophecy. If you want to get along with people, avoid negativity from all comers and live in the land of the positive. Throughout my years as a manager, I have always found that the root cause of malaise in any toxic work environment can be traced to one or two people. Experience has proven to me that if I eliminate the problem people, the rest of the staff will rally to bring happiness back into the workplace.

Let's look at some of the other issues that cause problems for people at work. Money, favoritism, promotions, hours of work, inability to perform, and a lack of mentoring, are all potential elements of a problematic workplace.

MONEY IS AN ESSENTIAL PART OF ANY JOB.

Hundreds or even thousands of analysts, consultants and business coaches will tell you that no one quits a job because of money. I would like to shatter that myth once and for all. Money is an essential element of any job. It is for the most part, the reason that people go to work in the first place. It is also a basic necessity for survival in civilized society. Beyond that, money is a method of keeping score. If an employee finds out that someone in their department with the same seniority and doing essentially the same job is paid more than him, his ego-based competitive human drive will kick in. He will feel hurt, betrayed, disappointed and angry. At that point, money will become the enabler to allow him to become toxic or quit. The fact that he is paid less than he feels he should be will provide him with justification for retaliation against his employer by whatever means he has at his disposal. If you are unhappy with your paycheck, do something about it. Talk to your employer first and if you cannot come to terms with him, find another job. Leave your current job on good terms and do not burn any bridges. Do not become a toxic, troublemaking employee. That kind of behavior will shatter your credibility, make your life more difficult than you can imagine, and prevent you from allowing everyone you meet to become a positive force in your life. Negativity begets negativity. Always approach each situation, *(yes, even money!)* with a positive attitude. In reality I seldom run across an employer who deliberately pays one employee less than another as a punitive measure. If two employees of equal responsibility and tenure are paid differently, it usually indicates a performance differential. If you are the one being paid less, make the first move and discuss your performance with your boss. If that discussion does not satisfy your needs, move on to another opportunity with grace and style. Getting along with people requires that you always take the high road and maintain decorum even in the face of strife or personal misfortune. Oh, and by the way, I must admit that the theory that people do not quit for money is correct in some cases. If the paycheck is suitable to her position, ability, performance, and tenure, then an employee who quits is in fact, probably not quitting for money. She may however use money as an excuse to avoid the confrontation that admitting to a deeper problem might bring.

HAVE YOU EVER NOTICED THAT SOME PEOPLE SPEND AN INORDINATE AMOUNT OF TIME *SUCKING UP* TO THE BOSS?

Have you ever witnessed favoritism in the workplace? I have. Often managers and supervisors will take a special interest in certain employees and treat them better than the others. This is a dangerous practice that takes place in many workplaces all over the world. People will be people and it is difficult even for a manager not to play favorites with people she considers friends, people she is related to or people that take a special interest in her. It makes perfect sense to me that bosses will take a special interest in friends and family. It is not a good thing, but there is little that can be done about it...but what about the others? Have you ever noticed that some people spend an inordinate amount of time *sucking up* to the boss? Have you noticed that some of your co-workers have many more compliments for the boss, than you ever thought imaginable? Occasionally those people get ahead in their companies at a faster rate than their less flattering counterparts even if they possess lesser talent. Unfortunately since managers are people, they tend to enjoy having their egos stroked and they also tend to respond favorably to people who provide them with positive reinforcement. Often those managers do not even recognize that the flatterer is *sucking up*. Since all they are hearing is positive reinforcement, they will bask in it and even believe that they are as good as the compliments would indicate. The positive reinforcement will draw them to that employee and since positivity breeds positivity, they will want to enable advancement and success for their admirer. You must ask yourself if what you are seeing is in fact inappropriate behavior and if you should waste any time thinking about it or reacting to it at all. People who spend a lot of time complimenting their superiors have a personality trait that requires them to subjugate themselves to the leader of the pack. In a wolf pack, there is one dominant male position. Various males do battle from time to time to claim the title of pack leader. Once the stronger male has won the crown, many of the younger and weaker males will display extreme compliance to his wishes including rolling onto their backs to expose their soft underbellies. That action indicates that they are subservient and willing to give up any defense they might have to the dominant male's wishes. The *sucking up* that some people do with their bosses is not unlike the subservience of the younger, weaker wolves. They are willing to put their pride and ego aside in order to gain the favor of the stronger, dominant boss. By showing vulnerability, they believe that they will improve their position in the firm just as the weaker wolves are trying to improve their position in the pack. They have decided to avoid being true to themselves in favor of a dishonest, self-serving approach. A smart boss will see through the advances of their supposed admirers and treat them the same as they would anyone else. My advice is to work hard and always do your best. Do not adopt a persona that you do not approve of by becoming a *suck up* yourself in order to fight fire with fire. Instead, work hard, stay true to yourself, be the best you can be and work like there is no tomorrow. Your diligence will be rewarded and your integrity will be intact. People with a strong sense of integrity have very little trouble getting along with other people and they are successful on many levels. *Suck ups* on the other hand, despite any workplace success they might achieve, are generally failures at life just as the weaker wolves will seldom become pack leaders. Folks who are not true to themselves tend to be universally disliked to the point that they have trouble getting along with many of the people that pass through their lives.

IF YOU WANT A PROMOTION, YOU NEED TO LET YOUR BOSS KNOW ABOUT IT.

It is a natural human desire to want to progress through a Company's hierarchy. People generally want the acknowledgement that comes with a promotion and their competitive nature drives them to seek advancement. The competition for promotions however, can cause resentment and negative behavior in the workplace. Those who are amply qualified to progress will acquire promotions with little or no effort. Those who are not as talented will have to work much harder to get ahead. If you want to get a promotion at work, try not to let your ego take advantage of your otherwise good nature. Insist on appropriate training and regular performance reviews to be certain that you are actually qualified for advancement. You cannot advance unless you have done the work that is required to get you there. Ask yourself, *"Have I done my best and is my best good enough?"* If your answer to either part of that question is no, then you are not ready for a promotion and you should accept that fact without becoming difficult or defensive. When you see someone else getting a promotion that you wanted, before becoming annoyed or frustrated, ask yourself if that person actually deserved it. Nine times out of ten if you are being realistic, you will accept the fact that the other person did in fact earn the promotion they received. If you want to get ahead, pay attention to workers or leaders that you admire. Watch them very closely and try to emulate them. It is a fact that successful people are successful for a reason. They do things in a certain way and they offer something that others do not. If you can follow their lead in any small way, you will be that much closer to your next promotion. Oh, and don't forget to ask! If you want a promotion, you need to let your boss know about it. Most promotions happen because of a change in staffing that frees up a position. If you are shy and retiring, your boss will have no idea that you want to progress at that moment in time. Many good people have been passed over time and time again because no one knew that they wanted advancement. If you are doing a good job, your employer's attitude might just be, *"let's leave well enough alone."* Don't assume that someone is watching you at all times and that your good work will be rewarded. A promotion often comes at least partially because of *self-promotion*. Blow your own horn from time to time to wake up the people at the top who can help you the most.

IF YOU THINK YOU ARE WORKING TOO HARD, YOU PROBABLY ARE.

I tend to be a *morning-person*. When I say that, I mean that my natural body rhythms favor the daylight hours. When I wake up in the morning I am ready to go and my energy levels are very high right through until about 2:00 PM. I tend to become sleepy later in the afternoon but I generally get a surge of energy around 4:00 PM that carries me for the balance of the day. I once had a sawmill job where I started at 3:00 PM and worked until 11:00 PM. They called it the afternoon shift. Because I was going to bed late after doing a lot of physical work, and getting up at a normal hour, but doing no work again until 3:00PM, my natural body rhythms were completely out of whack. Even though I was a healthy teenager at the time I was always fatigued. The same holds true for people who work unusually long hours. The reason that the workday is scheduled to approximately eight hours for each shift in most workplaces is because that is all the work that any normal person can effectively handle without a break. If you work longer than eight hours, your mind will not be functioning as well as it should and you will lose focus to the point that the quality and quantity of your work will suffer. In addition to poor work, your fatigue will impair your mood. Along with that, your behavior will be unusual to you and quite possibly repugnant to others. For that reason, I tend to avoid authorizing *overtime* if at all possible. The work that gets done during overtime periods is often less than acceptable in quality and quantity. If you think you are working too hard, you probably are. If you want to prevent personal frustration and physical fatigue, try to work no more than eight hours at a stretch. Don't be the martyr who sacrifices herself for the good of the team. Work hard during your regular shift and then go home. Your work will improve and your friends and loved ones will appreciate your better mood.

EVERYONE IS GOOD AT SOMETHING.

I get a bit annoyed with employers who chastise certain employees for poor performance without knowing the reason for it. I am a firm believer that nobody except someone who is desperately disturbed, wakes up in the morning with the intention of performing poorly. All normal people want to do a good job and everyone likes positive acknowledgement for a job well done. If my hypothesis is correct, why then do some people perform poorly? Firstly, poor performance is generally based on comparisons. We compare people to benchmarks set by our Companies or we compare them to other employees who are performing very well. In many cases, we expect extraordinary results from ordinary people. In other cases, a top performer might be so good at her job that it is impossible for the average mortal to even approach her standard. When we criticize people, we destroy their initiative and break their spirits. Unfortunately, once we have broken them down, our accusations of poor performance often become self-fulfilling prophecies. They will stop trying and at that point their performance level will drop even lower than their natural capability would allow. Everyone is good at something. It is important for employers to understand that and realize that if they have an underperforming employee, they have either trained them inadequately or they have placed them in the wrong job. If a person is not able to utilize his natural talents and do something that interests him, the best that can be expected is mediocre results. On the other hand, people who are lucky enough to be able to do what they have a natural ability for, will excel. That is what I refer to as, ***Right Person-Right Job.*** Employers should have the courage to tell employees about their underperformance and if it is not a training issue, they should endeavor to find out what they might be good at. If there is no job in the employer's workplace that suits the underperforming employee they should set them free to seek out employment that is more suitable. Employees too, share in the responsibility for underperformance. If you are not performing as well as another employee, you should find out why. Don't fight the fact or make excuses for it. Attempt to emulate stronger performers and make sure you have the knowledge and skills to do your job. If you come to the conclusion that you are simply incapable of performing at a high level, get out of that job as soon as you can. There is something in the world that you can excel at, so seek it out and be happy. When you are doing what you enjoy doing everyday, your life will be enriched, your mood will be perennially good, and your confidence level will be *through the roof.* At that point, you will radiate happiness and you will find that getting along with people is incredibly easy.

IF THERE IS NO MENTORSHIP PROGRAM AT YOUR WORKPLACE, CREATE YOUR OWN.

Many employers do not understand the value of mentoring in the workplace. New employees and employees who change positions need the support of someone well experienced in the job to assist them in becoming proficient. Mentors also tend to support and encourage new employees in order to make them valuable team members. A mentor should be someone who is truly interested in helping people and if possible, it is advisable to match the personality type of the mentor with the personality of the person being mentored. If the mentor and his protégé are not matched perceptually, the mentoring will fail to produce good results. Most workplaces have a number of people employed who will gladly give of their own time to help others. All too often, the process of mentoring is considered a waste of time or it is assumed that employees will automatically take new employees into the fold and work with them. Unfortunately that does not always happen. Employees are busy doing their own work and the introduction of a new employee is often viewed as a hindrance. A formal mentorship program should be introduced into every workplace. If there is no mentorship program at your workplace, create your own. Find someone who is skilled and well respected in your field, and make a friend of her. Do what she does and ask her for help when you are in trouble. You will be a better employee for it and your performance will be better than it will be if you go it alone. When you become a high performer, you too will be able to mentor others and feel the joy of being instrumental in the growth and personal development of someone else. Mentorship is the ultimate in getting along with people. Groups of people who know their jobs well and are cognizant of where they fit in the organization are happy groups that get along well.

I started off this chapter by saying, ***"It's just work, People."*** I think that is also a great way to end it. If you want to be happier, more productive and a joy to be around, you must accept the fact that your work is only a small part of who you are. The art of getting along with people requires a balance amongst work, home, and social life.

What did we learn in Chapter Seven?

- Work can bring on physical symptoms of stress.

- People who are not happy at work often produce poor quality results.

- Obsession with work is not healthy.

- Money matters. It is a way of keeping score.

- Don't be a *suck-up*. People who are not true to themselves are often universally disliked.

- If you want a promotion, tell somebody.

- Overwork creates poor quality results.

- For good quality results the right people need to be doing the right jobs.

- Mentorship in the workplace is important.

- In order to be happy we all need balance in our work, social, and home lives.

I LOVE THIS PLACE. I JUST HATE THE PEOPLE HERE!

"Whenever you put a bunch of people together you run the risk of a war breaking out"

CHAPTER 8

Whether it is at work, in the neighborhood, or at the Rotary club, whenever people choose to spend time together, they inevitably begin to find fault with the group they have chosen. If they don't dislike the entire, collective group, you can bet there is someone in the group they don't like. Why is that? Think about it and ask yourself why people simply cannot walk into a room full of people and have totally positive thoughts about everyone there. Or more importantly, think about the reasons that *you* have negative feelings about other people. Pick one person and ask yourself if the reasons you came up with merit the grief you are causing yourself and that person. Unless the person you dislike stole your car or beat you half to death for no apparent good reason, I believe that with a little effort you can probably put your negativity on the back burner and start to get along with him. In fact, I recommend that you go through this process every time you run into someone you don't get along with. You will find that eventually you will have a lot more friends and will find yourself getting along with a lot more people. Oh sure, there are people you will never get along with, but there are many more that you will if you try a little harder.

WORSHIP, IN AND OF ITSELF, IS CERTAINLY NOT BAD.

Let's think about war again. The people of France fought a religious war between the Catholics, (Huguenots) and Protestants that went on for over thirty years during the fifteen hundreds (1562 to 1598). Those were people who lived in the same country, worshipped the same God and read from the same Good Book. Although their religion was based on the same basic principles and both accepted Jesus as the Son of God, they were both so attached to their own dogma that they chose to kill each other in order to promote their respective forms of worship. It is apparent that the Royalty in France felt the protestant reformers were in fact a threat to the state and therefore a threat to their continued rein. I suspect that the religious leaders duped the people of France. While the commoners were fighting to preserve their religious views, the Huguenot and Protestant leaders were fighting for control of the country. The war although based in religion, became a power struggle between two powerful factions who thought little of God while raising their swords to their fellow countrymen. I don't want it to appear that I am picking on Christianity. The French religious war represents only one of many religious wars that have occurred in various parts of the world since the dawn of mankind.

Many human beings need to worship a God or Gods and they almost always select a single leadership idol such as Jesus or Mohammed. Human beings need leaders for almost everything they do and in their respective cultures Jesus and Mohammed have been chosen to lead people to their own particular version of Heaven. They are the official representatives of God and Allah. Even though both of these leaders appear to have been deeply peaceful, their followers were able to justify warfare and bloodshed in their name. Worship, in and of itself, is certainly not bad. However, when people use it as an excuse to kill each other I cannot help but feel betrayal and disappointment. Religious wars amply illustrate the fact that whenever you put two or more people together with a common goal, no matter how just and righteous the cause, there is a good chance a war will break out.

Those of us fortunate enough to live in non-war faring cultures, must be on guard not to become involved in skirmishes of our own. Schoolyard fistfights amongst children occur every day due to the primeval tendencies of human beings. Even at an early age some human kids, like wolves, feel an overwhelming need to dominate the pack. They will risk disciplinary action or even expulsion while taking on all comers in order to be known as the toughest kid in school or just to prove a point. The violence currently being experienced in schools should not exist. North America has centuries of experience and has invested billions of dollars in research, training, and rehabilitation techniques in its never-ending effort to prevent violence. None of it is working. Violence in schools has erupted to the point that in some schools children have to pass through metal detectors and have their guns and knives confiscated before they go to class! What's with that? Why have all of our efforts to make human beings act in a civilized fashion gone unheeded? More importantly, what chance do those pistol-packing kids have to become happy, productive adults in the future? How can we possibly expect them to ever get along with other people? What kind of world will we see in the next few decades if we don't curtail the violence now? Television, print media, the internet, and even radio all promote violence, bad behavior, and rebellion against authority in the name of good entertainment. You can't change that overnight but nor should you use it as an excuse to accept what is happening to our kids.

HEE, HEE! MOM IS NEVER GOING TO PUNISH ME!

None of us can single-handedly stop a train that is hurtling downhill. However, any one of us can change our behavior and improve our own attitude in order to make a difference in our immediate environment. We can also teach our children to be good and kind, and we can discipline them positively at an early age when we find them breaking the rules that we have given them. Indulgence and acceptance of reprehensible behavior will not work. Too often I find rude, nasty, violent children being excused or defended by their parents after they have committed a reprehensible act. Too often I see a parent telling a child that she will punish him if he does the reprehensible act again. Then, when the child does it again, the parent threatens him again. In retaliation, the child does it again. This cycle sometime goes on for hours without the parent ever actually punishing the child at all. What do you think the child is thinking? He is thinking, *"Hee, Hee! Mom is never going to punish me! I can get away with anything!"* Not only is the child freely exercising his primeval, competitive need to *win*…he is also learning that bad behavior carries no consequences. If the lack of consequences carries on for any length of time, that same child will carry his lack of respect for authority with him well into adulthood. Taken to the worst extreme a child with indulgent, ineffective parents may become a violent child or a criminal adult. I suppose I may be wandering into dangerous territory with many of my readers who have children, but I have to say that kids brought up without effective discipline often have problems getting along with people in later life. If you want your children to get along with others for a lifetime, follow through with your promises of discipline and be consistent in the enforcement of your rules. It may seem difficult and heartless at the time, but you will be thrilled with the results in the long run. Oh, and the bonus: your friends and family will want to spend more time with you if you have well-disciplined, respectful children. Nobody likes to be in the company of spoiled, insolent, noisy brats for very long! If you are disappointed that your generous barbeque invitations are often avoided or ignored, the problem might be right under your nose. By the way, I am not going to tell you what form of discipline you should use. That information is for another author and another book.

I am talking about children because they will eventually inherit the earth. What they do with it will depend largely on what we do with them now. I am also being a tad selfish. When I finally retire, your kids will be running my world and I want them to be kind and compassionate to all of my old cronies and me. We will still be in the world, driving too slow and spending far too much time asking how things work. We will always get in the way of young folks in a hurry and we will assume that our old ways of doing things would work much better than the new fangled ways. My message to old folks is this: *"The current batch of young people **will** take over the world!"* They have no choice. Those of you who think that they cannot possibly run the world unless they change are wrong. In every past generation young people have taken over the world and made it their own. That is called progress, and I thank God for it. If we hadn't allowed young people to change the world to suit them in the past you would probably be reading this book by candlelight. Having said all of that, wouldn't it be great if the next crop of adults could make the world a nicer place than it is now?

A NEGATIVE REACTION TO SOME PEOPLE IS NATURAL AND COMMONPLACE IN MANKIND.

Let's get back to the Rotary club. Human beings are social animals. They have an innate need to live together in communities and to socialize and communicate with each other on a regular basis. That is why we have a need for cities, neighborhoods, businesses and clubs. One would think that since the need for social interaction is predetermined, the need for harmonious relationships would be a natural byproduct of that need. In fact, we know the opposite is often true. It is clear that people often get along poorly without any apparent provocation. We have uncovered some of the reasons for that throughout this book. When you walk into the hotel ballroom for your early morning Rotary meeting, you are probably hoping that a certain person isn't there; that *so-and-so* doesn't sit with you; or that some other person doesn't talk too much. As rational and fair as you would generally like to be, in any regular and repeated social situation you will develop prejudices against some people. You will often want to mask your prejudice in order to protect your air of integrity but your aura will give your real feelings away to the people you don't like...and to others. A negative reaction to some people is natural and commonplace in mankind. Human beings simply cannot like everyone, trust everyone or agree with everyone all of the time. The best we can hope for is a semblance of order that allows our business and social lives to move forward with nothing more than occasional, minor, people-based setbacks.

If you want to enjoy life and remove a lot of the stress from your time on earth, try changing the way you view other people and then adjust your behavior accordingly. When you find a person repugnant for whatever reason, simply ignore the source of your annoyance. It is only when you allow the actions of people to infiltrate your mind and soul that they can affect you negatively. If you begin to accept that their negative behavior can be restricted to them and others who buy into it, you will rise above it and become immune to its effects. You have the right to choose which people and what information you allow into your life. With effort, those things that offend you can be avoided or ignored. You need not allow unpleasantness into your life and you may reject anything that you find offensive. If you are a person of strong character and irrefutable integrity, (something we should all strive for) you can rest easy in the knowledge that your actions are beyond reproach. If you are comfortable with your own character and satisfied that your course of action is fair, the negativity of others will have no impact on you. You will be *bullet proof!*

YOU ARE UNIQUE, AND IN YOUR OWN WAY YOU ARE SPECIAL.

While you are working on your attitude toward others, remember that they do not live in your head or your heart. Nobody thinks about things the way you do. You are unique, and in your own way you are special. You are an individual, but you are not right all the time and your perceptions do not necessarily represent what other people perceive. Do not expect people to live up to your standards. Your standards may be completely repugnant to others and their view of you may be as negative as your view of them. I just gasped while writing this as I thought of the utter futility of so many people in the world attempting to force other people to live by the standards that they have set for themselves. People actually get into raging arguments over political parties; rock videos; merlot versus cabernet; and whether or not Generation *X* works harder than Generation *Y*. You hear it every day: *"You should do this!" "They should do that!" "He shouldn't have done it like that!" "Why would anyone think like that?" "What a stupid thing to do!"* People are judging and criticizing each other constantly. I recently got into a minor argument with a client who was adamant that if the younger generation did not smarten up and work harder, the world would fall into wrack and ruin. As a major employer of young people, he was completely unimpressed with the work ethic of his employees and fed up with attempting to manage them. Although I understood his concerns, I felt the need to point out that the younger generation did not have to change to suit us because they will eventually be the older generation that will inherit the earth, whether we like it or not. I also pointed out that it was employers who would probably have to change to suit the needs and wants of Generation Y. After all, they are the largest employee group in North America and subsequently wield a lot of power in the workforce. When I realized that he was actually becoming quite angry with me because of what I was saying, I changed my tack and softened my approach. Rather than vehemently forcing my point of view, I admitted that I might be wrong and asked him how he envisioned the world in the future. I offered genuine interest in his point of view and spoke with the greatest of respect for his experience and expertise. He could see that I was not interested in doing battle with him and after some reflection, he declared that it was probably time he retired. He also admitted to me that his views were *old school,* and possibly not congruent with current management practices. The bottom line is that he realized that he wanted the world to change to suit his own personal views, but in the course of our conversation it came to him that he probably would not be able to make that happen. You will find getting along with people much easier if you listen carefully to their point of view and if they are convinced of it, don't try to force your own opposing perspective. Let the ideas of other folks live and you will find that they will want to get along with you. The great thing is that because people are inherently generous, when they feel that they have been heard they will be more interested in hearing your ideas as well. Fair and honest consideration of other people's perspectives is essential to getting along with people. Often, the harder you try to be right, the more you will seem wrong in the eyes of others.

THERE ARE MANY REASONS FOR BEING NICE AT ALL TIMES.

Can't you just be *nice*? You have probably heard that a thousand times. It **does** work, you know. Despite your possible rejection of the notion of being nice to all of the people, all of the time, I can assure you that a nice, polite, respectful demeanor will open up opportunities to you that may otherwise remain hidden. Tact matters and there is no replacement for good manners. Nice people are successful. Some are rich; some are poor; and some are just average on the financial scale. Their real success is not in their bank accounts…it is in the pure joy and fulfillment that envelops their lives. Nice people seldom argue and they never fight. They are not targets for criticism or defamation and they don't have to worry about being embarrassed publicly for negative acts. They are good and they are kind and the world knows it. Hundreds, and in some cases, thousands of people will show up at a funeral for a *nice guy*. Very few people will show up at a funeral for a cynical, *grumpy-Gus*. Nice people are happy more often than not. Medical science shows that people who are generally happy live longer, healthier lives than folks who are generally angry, depressed or stressed. There are many reasons for being nice at all times. Just try it. You just might like it and you will certainly find that getting along with people is easier.

By the way, if your neighbor plays her music too loud or her dog barks all night, you need not harbor a grudge and give her dirty looks for the next fifteen years! Instead, go over to her house and have a chat with her. Don't yell across the fence in anger, or leave a nasty anonymous note in her mailbox. Go to her front door and ask if you can have a conversation with her about the things that have been bothering you. By taking a direct, reasoned approach you will avoid the inevitable retaliation that would occur if you acted with impulsive rage. When she answers the door, don't adopt a deliberately nasty look or speak with obvious anger. Do not accuse and do not blame. Simply state your case and ask if there is anything she can do to alleviate the stress you are feeling because of her actions. Most normal human beings will react positively to a calm, rational request for assistance with a relatively easy-to-solve problem. Open, honest communication is one of the best ways to make the best of a bad situation. During all potentially inflammatory discussions, think about your comments in advance and make a pact with yourself to control your emotions. The minute you lose your composure and begin to attack another person, the war will be on and any chance you might have had for a peaceful conclusion will evaporate into thin air. In war, there are always casualties and there are no real winners. Emotional fights with friends, neighbors, and relatives are like the attack on Pearl Harbor during World War II. The bombing victims lost the battle but the invading forces that bombed and strafed their unsuspecting opponents prior to a formal declaration of war did not win the hearts of anyone. The enemy had a decisive but hollow victory that day. It will always be remembered as one of the most horrific and unacceptable acts of war in the history of the world. It was also the beginning of the end for Japan. Any time you declare war and drop an emotional bomb on another human being without extreme provocation or advance warning, you can expect to suffer, no matter what the outcome. Think before you speak and exercise impeccable integrity when you confront a difficult situation.

If you want to enjoy the company of everyone in your life, you must put your ego on the back burner and avoid starting a war at all costs. Getting along with people is all up to you.

What did we learn in Chapter Eight?

- People often find fault with members of their own chosen group.

- Whenever you bring two or more people together with a common goal, no matter how just and righteous the cause, there is a good chance a war will break out.

- It is possible to change our own behavior and raise our children to think differently about other people.

- You need not allow unpleasantness into your life and you may reject anything that you find offensive.

- You are an individual, but you are not right all the time.

- Nice people are happy healthy people.

- Think before you speak, control your emotions, be direct and exercise impeccable integrity when you confront a potentially difficult situation.

- If you want to get along with people you must put your ego on the back burner and avoid starting a war at all costs. It's all up to you.

IS THERE A MODEL
IN THE HOUSE?

*"If you want to get along with someone,
think like them; act like them; be like them."*

CHAPTER 9

Great salesmen know a lot about modeling. For them, modeling is what they have to do to make a sale. When they are with a prospective client, they listen very closely to what the prospect is saying and they pay close attention to his or her mannerisms. People naturally bond with other people who are much like them. A good salesman will do everything he can to understand what makes his client tick and will then adapt his own behavior to model as closely as possible the behavior of his client. In addition, a good salesman will probe for information about what the client is interested in. For example, does he like to talk about baseball, politics, automobiles, or science fiction? Once he has an idea of what interests the client on a personal level, he will focus on those things during his chatty preamble to the sale. As a salesman myself for a large part of my career, I always found that I had the greatest success and the least amount of resistance from people who were most like me. Those who had the same interests as me, had a similar sense of humor as mine, and enjoyed the same amount of informational detail as me, seemed to trust me more than those who were completely different than me. Contrary to the old romantic adage, opposites do NOT attract. If it happens that people who are intellectual polar opposites become physically attracted to each other, they will have a short-lived romance. The same holds true for an overbearing, pushy salesman who tries to sell to a shy, reticent buyer. He might make the first sale but the buyer will run for the hills the next time the salesman calls.

YOU CANNOT FORCE SOMEONE TO APPRECIATE YOUR INTERESTS.

Not unlike the sales arena, people are constantly selling themselves to each other outside of work as well. When you are introduced to someone at the Rotary club or the PTA meeting, you will immediately put on a smile and hold out your hand in an effort to make physical contact during the obligatory handshake ritual. At the moment your hand touches his and you feel the relative warmth or coolness of his flesh you will have begun to size him up as a potential friend, business contact, or love mate. If your feelings are positive, you will want him to like you. If you are good at modeling you will begin to observe his mannerisms and listen for clues to what he is interested in. With great luck his interests will be similar to yours and you will quite naturally strike up a stimulating conversation. If you have little in common, you will have to work a lot harder at getting along with him. You will have to pay very close attention to what he says and show great interest in his activities and accomplishments. If you have absolutely nothing in common or his interests, activities, and accomplishments are offensive to you, it is time to walk away and find someone else to bond with. By the way, don't work too hard to make yourself interesting to someone who is clearly not interested in what you are saying. You cannot force someone to appreciate your interests. If you try, the relationship might end abruptly before it has a chance to begin.

To become better at modeling, it helps to understand how motivation and behavior occurs in people in the first place. Everyone has basic, underlying needs for certain things in their lives. Modern behaviorists have boiled all of those human motivations down to just six elements. Different organizations use different monikers for them but regardless of what they are called, they generally fit into the following categories:

-**Traditional:** A need for a system for living.

-**Social:** A need for fairness, equality, and compassion for all of mankind.

-**Utilitarian:** A need for money, possessions, and a good return on investment.

-**Individualistic:** A need for power and control.

-**Theoretical**: A need for knowledge.

-**Aesthetic:** A need for beauty and harmony in life.

Human beings are attracted to, repelled by, or indifferent to all of these motivations. The more a person is attracted to any one of them, the more it will become part of her persona and something that she can easily be identified by. Just as an obsession with any one of these motivations is easily identifiable, so is repulsion or indifference to any of them. For example, a person who has a high **utilitarian** motivation might spend most of her life seeking ever-increasing amounts of money and expensive personal items. If that same person is also highly **individualistic** they may own their own business or be involved in politics. If they are low **utilitarian** and low **individualistic** they will be annoyed with people who seek great wealth and they will have an aversion to politics. If they are indifferent to or repulsed by the **traditional** motivation, they probably don't go to church and will tend to accept change very readily...they prefer not to live their lives by any set system. Highly **traditiona**l people tend to be quite spiritual and need a consistent system for living. Because of the myriad of potential motivations and non-motivations that people have in their hearts and minds, this is a very complex subject...just as people are complex beings. However, it is safe to say that if you understand the motivations of people it is easier to model them and much easier to get along with them. Since I began studying these theories, I have become more adept at understanding people and getting along with them. Interestingly, because I tend to be quite high on the **theoretical** scale I have a great desire to learn everything I can about people. If I was low on the **theoretical** scale, I would probably have very little interest in *why* people are the way they are. I would simply accept them for *what* they are.

BEHAVIOR IS OUR EXTERNAL, VISIBLE REACTION TO EVENTS AND SITUATIONS.

The methods we humans use to achieve, acquire, and create the things that our *motivations* tell us we want is known as *behavior*. Behavior is our external, visible reaction to events and situations. Hence, when we wake up in the morning our motivations are with us and we have an irresistible desire to go out into the world to achieve, acquire and create everything that our psyche tells us we want to have or be involved with. In other words our motivations are what we want and our behavior is what we do to get what we want. Behaviorists have boiled basic human behavior down to only 4 elements. As in the case of motivations, various organizations use different terms for them but generally they will fit into the following categories:

-Dominant: This can be identified by forceful, confident, and often angry, behavior.

-Influencing: This can be identified by happy, optimistic, trusting, and outgoing behavior.

-Steady: This can be identified by sociable, insecure, thoughtful, and sometimes fearful behavior.

-Compliant: This can be identified by organized, tidy, careful behavior with a consistent need for, and observance of rules.

All people will exhibit elements of all 4 behaviors from time to time. In fact there will usually be a blend of all of the behaviors at most times. During times of stress or danger, people will generally focus more on one behavior than another. For example, a person with a generally balanced behavioral personality who finds himself facing an angry grizzly bear during an ill-fated hiking trip will have to make some important decisions in a hurry. A more *dominant* person might challenge the bear, yelling, screaming and threatening it in order to make it run away. A person with a high *influencing* level, might talk to the bear with a joyful voice or even sing to it as he backs away. A person with high *steadiness* would probably say or do nothing…paralyzed with fear he would mentally consider many, many options as the bear advanced toward him. A *compliant* person would mentally run through all of the information they had ever seen or read about what to do when in the presence of a wild bear and would follow their learning to the tee. None of the responses is wrong or right. I have used this example to illustrate why everyone in the world responds differently when presented with similar stimulus. The same holds true for work, home, and social situations. The reason we get along or don't get along with people is our varying behavior. *Influencing* people are full of fun and optimism. They make a point of getting along with almost everyone and are often the centre of attention. *Dominant* people are forceful and want to be in charge of almost every situation. If they don't get their way, they often become angry. *Steady* people tend to be quiet and pensive but are very friendly when approached. *Compliant* people want to follow all of the rules and tend to be obsessive about tidiness and organization.

When a behavioral element is very low, it produces the opposite effect of a higher one. In other words, people who are low dominant are fearful and reserved while high dominants are courageous and bold. Low influencers are pessimistic, untrusting and quiet, while high influencers are optimistic, trusting and loud. Low steady's are in a hurry, while high steadies would like to slow the world down. Folks with low compliance will have no use whatsoever for rules and authority, while those with high compliance will follow rules to a fault.

Because behavior is always a blend of the four elements, you will find that a person who is highly dominant and highly compliant at the same time will insist that the rules be followed at all times and will fight anyone who tries to do things differently. High influencers with low compliance will usually be quite silly since they have no concern for society's rules and want to be the center of attention. A person who is low steady and low compliant will make decisions very quickly with almost no consideration for society's rules. People are complex and there is a lifetime of information that you can study to find out what makes them all tick. The important thing is that you care enough about getting along with people to try to figure them out so that you can get along with them. Even without studying behavioral science, you can understand people and get along with them much better by paying attention to their reactions and amending your behavior to suit them.

LISTENING IS THE MOST IMPORTANT ELEMENT OF VERBAL COMMUNICATION.

As I said earlier, you are not always right and you need to hear what another person is saying if you want to get along with him. Listening is the most important element of verbal communication. When in the presence of another person, listen, listen, and listen some more! Not only will you learn something that you have never heard before, but you will gain insight into the soul of your discussion partner. I find that too many people are far too enamored of the sound of their own voice and the brilliance of their own accomplishments and opinions. I was like that myself in my younger years. Now, when I enter into any kind of conversation, I tend to hang back and listen for quite a long time before I offer my own opinion or voice any concerns I might have. The older I get, the more I learn about people, and the more I find it easy to get along with them. Of course there are still some people whose behaviors, attitudes, and opinions are so inflammatory or simply repugnant to me that I must make the choice not to get along with them. Fortunately, those people are few and far between.

Once you have listened to someone you will be in a much better position to communicate with her. Once you feel that you have her sorted out, model the content of your conversation in a fashion that will appeal to her. If she speaks quietly and slowly, do not speak quickly and loudly. If she wants to talk about the composition of a Monet painting, do not change the subject to hockey. If she has clear-cut views that the criminal justice system is too soft on murderers, and you don't agree, do not immediately tell her she is wrong. In this instance, there is a potential for a lot of lively disagreement and it could become an acrimonious, relationship-ending discussion. The natural instinct of many people is to force the discussion to move in the direction they want it to, rather than gently but deliberately shifting it toward their way of thinking. If you ask questions, instead of making statements, you will begin to hear a change in the attitude of the other person. In the case at hand, ask her how the justice system should handle murderers. Ask how she would handle murderers if she were totally responsible for dispensing justice to them. Instead of saying, *"I don't think any human being has the right to take the life of another!"*…try saying, *"So how do you feel about the concept that two wrongs don't make a right? I recently read that the majority of Western people feel that the death penalty is not acceptable in modern civilization."* By making it a question and basing it in the feelings of others, you will have taken away the appearance that you have launched an attack on her. You will have made a conscious decision not to make it personal for her and she will now be in a better position to consider your point of view, instead of defending her own.

FOR DOMINANT PEOPLE, WINNING IS ALL IMPORTANT.

When you are trying to get along with an extremely dominant individual it is often best to let them win when they become adamant. If you completely disagree with her perspective and model your behavior to be as dominant as hers, there can be no winners. In all likelihood a war will break out. I find that when I am in the presence of a highly dominant person, if I let her win one argument, I can usually convince her to let me have my way with something else. For dominant people winning is all important. However like everyone else, they take pleasure in helping other people accomplish their goals. Because of their need to win, there is a good chance they will take credit for any good that comes from any situation they might help you with. However, if you can put your ego aside and accept that the important thing was getting what you wanted, the fact that the dominant person took credit for it will be unimportant to you.

The other personality types require special treatment as well. When you are dealing with highly influential people expect them to talk far too much and attempt humor at every opportunity. They are highly expressive and they love people. They are perhaps the easiest of all types to get along with. However, if you are a compliant person, you will soon tire of their lack of concern for detail and if you are a high steady you may be put off by the speed at which they make decisions. Dominants will easily control them and they are usually fine with that. If you want to get along with a high influential, let them talk and always laugh at their jokes.

High steady's are addicted to security and tend to want a lot of information before making a decision. They want assurance that any decision they make is the right one before they act on it. They are committed to their families and they strive to provide safety and security for them. They prefer not to make a decision unless their family members are aware of it and buy into it. They generally want the world to slow down, so don't push them too hard to make a decision or force them to create speedy results. The expression, *"Slow and steady wins the race."* was undoubtedly written by a high steady personality.

Highly compliant people need rules for living. Unlike steady people they will make decisions quickly if they know that all of the rules and regulations have been followed. Obsessed with details, if you want to get along with them, come prepared with a lot of well-organized information and proof that what you are saying is correct. Do not try to get a high compliant person to change his mind unless you can prove that you are right. In conversation you can usually hold their attention with spreadsheets and mathematics. Most of the good accountants I know are high compliant but interestingly you will also find them in the fields of aviation and diesel repair. Anything that contains complex processes or formulas will hold their interest.

EVERY PERSON WILL NOT LIKE YOU THE WAY YOU ARE.

You may think that modeling is somewhat manipulative. That's because it is definitely very manipulative! It is *not* however, malicious. People are negotiating, capitulating and playing *mind games* with each other all the time. You are reading this book so that you can learn some better ways of getting along with people. In order to do that, you will have to accept that if you want to be popular and have more good relationships, you must stop listening to your ego and begin listening, negotiating, and capitulating with other people on a regular basis. Every person will simply not like you the way you are. You will have to find ways to make yourself more interesting and attractive to people if you want to get along with them. You will have to be willing to let them take the lead in conversations, win some arguments, exercise their egos, and play some mind games from time to time. Don't worry about it. If you have a genuine, heartfelt intention to get along with people it will all be worth it. Your life will be fulfilled and your stress levels will be greatly reduced. Once you decide to make a concerted effort to get along with everyone you meet, your persona will greatly improve. Eventually, the people you allow into your life will become totally intrigued with you and will want to be more like you. They will in fact start modeling themselves after you. I have seen it happen many times and I am confident that with diligence, modeling is one of the greatest relationship tools available to us. Getting along with people is easy with a small amount of extra effort.

What did we learn in Chapter Nine?

- Good salesmen use modeling to make sales.

- Everybody is selling himself or herself to someone else all of the time.

- There are six basic elements of human motivation.

- There are four basic elements of human behavior.

- The most important part of communication is listening.

- Speak in a similar fashion to the person you want to get along with and discuss things they want to hear.

- In the case of a disagreement, ask questions instead of making statements.

- Modeling is manipulative but not malicious.

IT TAKES ALL KINDS
TO MAKE A WORLD.

"Each person on earth prefers a different brand of poison. Some prefer more poison than others!"

CHAPTER 10

In this chapter we are going to explore the most common barriers to getting along with people. We will consider the good and bad in people and the best ways to deal with both. We will ponder whether or not certain types of behavior should be tolerated along with when and if you should just turn the other cheek and walk away. I will identify some of my favorite types of unacceptable behavior and provide some clues for getting along with people who exhibit them.

This chapter is filled with my personal opinions. With any luck you will agree with some of them. Any that you don't agree with will make you think…and that is a good thing. Getting along with people requires a lot of deep thought and a good deal of positive energy.

RUDE PEOPLE

RUDE PEOPLE are perhaps the hardest people of all for the majority of people on earth to get along with. The word *rude* has many definitions.

My thesaurus has several synonyms for it. They include *impolite, foul, vulgar, tasteless, offensive, crude, bad, improper, naughty, coarse, bad mannered,* and *indecent*. Folks who are rude tend to be insulting and offensive to others to the point that many people want to get away and stay away from them. Considering the twelve terms just noted, ask yourself if you are ever rude. Do you ever give people a reason to want to get away from you simply because of your behavior? Now that you are thinking about your own potential rudeness, let's consider how you can improve your relationships with the rude people around you.

You must understand *why* a person is rude before you can begin to deal with him or her. Some people are rude because they have a dismal lack of social awareness. They simply do not understand that the behavior they exhibit to others is offensive or personally insulting. When rude people are being vulgar, naughty or indecent for example, they are often attempting to be funny. They do not possess an adequate awareness of basic social etiquette to recognize that they have crossed the line and entered into the field of rudeness. Often, these are not bad people and they do not wish to be malicious or harmful in any way. In order to deal with them, you must be open and honest. You must tell them candidly that their behavior is unacceptable to you and that they must change their approach if they want to have any sort of relationship with you. It takes courage to deal with rude people. Be kind and understanding, but firm in the delivery of your message. Two negatives do not make a positive, and a nasty, angry approach will only set up a defensive response that will make the situation even worse. Most commonly you can expect an apologetic or humble reaction to your honesty. However, in the worst cases you might find that the rude person will become defensive and attack you with a barrage of rude behavior. She might even tell you that you have no sense of humor and that you should lighten up. Explain to her that your sense of humor is in fact different and that you do not wish to hear anymore of hers. At that point you will have planted the seed of reason, which will provide one of two possible outcomes: The rude person will either moderate her behavior in the future, or in retaliation she might continue on as she was prior to your discussion. Personal experience tells me that in the majority of cases, the rudeness will disappear during future encounters. In the best-case scenario it will enlighten the rude person to the point that they will moderate their behavior with everyone they meet. By the way, never give up. Just because you are unsuccessful in reducing or eliminating the rudeness of one person, do not assume that you will not be able to make a difference in someone else.

The same procedure will work for abrupt people, nasty people, and crude people. They all have specific reasons for their rude behavior and it helps to feel them out to determine just what it is that drives them. Once you have an idea of that, or even if you are never really able to understand their motivation, confront them with your concerns and give them the opportunity to improve. If they continue to behave badly, you can continue to attempt to help them or you can simply avoid them. If you feel that they want to improve but simply do not have adequate cognizance of good social behavior, you can help with coaching. Some very good people simply do not understand rudeness. Explain to them why their behavior is repugnant to others. Give them examples of good behavior and examples of good people they can emulate. If you take a genuine interest in them and they sense your desire to help, you might be able to turn them around completely. Eliminating rudeness in an adult is tough. It will take diligence and determination but it is worth it if you care about the person you want to help.

The worst thing you can do when dealing with a rude person is to become rude yourself. When faced with obnoxious behavior, the primeval, competitive human forces that reside within all of us will naturally come rushing to the surface. Before we know it, we might find ourselves reacting with anger and not thinking or caring about the appropriateness of our response. The reason for our retaliation is that human beings tend to take things personally when challenged in any way. We often take the negative behavior of others as a personal attack even if the behavior is not pointed directly at us. When we feel attacked, we feel the need to defend ourselves. Because we will lean toward an irrational, rather than reasoned response when under attack, we often end up with a negative result. When that happens, we will probably never be able to get along with our attackers. In most cases rudeness is not a deliberate attack on anyone. It is rather, a display of poor social awareness.

When faced with rudeness you need to *chill!* The first thing you should do before reacting is to think about what you are feeling and why you are feeling that way. Once you understand exactly what it is about the other person's behavior that you find offensive, consider whether or not it is as important an offence as you are making it out to be. In other words, consider whether it is worth a fight or if it is something you can simply let go. If for example, the person is using a lot of foul language and your value system tells you that foul language is inappropriate, do not take the tack of announcing publicly, in a loud voice that the person's foul language is disgusting. Public admonishment will serve no other purpose than to embarrass and anger the foul-mouthed person. His reaction to being embarrassed may be much worse than his original sin of swearing. At the very least he will have another reason to be annoyed with you. As mentioned earlier, consider why the person is being rude and then develop a reasoned course of action to deal with it. The best way to deal with it is always a private, one on one discussion.

Unless you are incredibly resilient and determined, you will never get along with everyone, so don't beat yourself up if you are unable to initiate any sort of significant change in every rude person you meet. However, if you can change just one of them, you will have made a positive difference in the world.

CONCEITED PEOPLE

CONCEITED PEOPLE are not at all easy to get along with for most of us. My thesaurus gives the following synonyms for the word, conceited: *self-important, proud, vain, smug, arrogant, high and mighty, stuck-up, snobbish,* and *self-satisfied.* Wow! There are lots of ways for conceited people to exhibit their own love of themselves. In essence, it is clear that some folks with a high level of self-esteem also have a need to let other people know about it. Bragging is a common symptom of conceit. In order to feed their self-esteem, conceited people speak loudly and often about their accomplishments and possessions. They are the center of the universe unto themselves just as they are a pain in the butt to everyone else!

Be careful during your own conversations that you too are not guilty of bragging. Always maintain a degree of humility when discussing your accomplishments. Try to avoid over-utilizing the words, *"I"* and *"Me"* when discussing the things you have done. Don't be one of those people who always seem to be saying, *"Look at me, look at me!"* People who spend a lot of time talking about what they have done in grandiose terms tend to annoy their listeners. Most of us are interested in finding out about other people but when they make every discussion about them; their strengths, accomplishments, and greatness, they soon become universally known as *conceited*. Conceited people are lonely people so tread lightly when speaking of your accomplishments. There is a fine line between pride and conceit. Consistent or constant bragging is usually where the line is crossed. If you actually believe you are better than someone else you will appear conceited to that person. If you believe you are better than entire groups of people you will seem generally conceited. If you are concerned that you might appear conceited to others from time to time, do a mental checklist right now to determine if you feel superior to others. If your list is even one person, bring yourself back to earth and accept that we are all just flesh and blood and given the right circumstances, anyone can be as good as anyone else.

Do not confuse self-esteem with conceit. People with a high level of self-esteem do not necessarily appear to be conceited. Those are the confident, self-assured people that other good folks look up to. Self-esteem is good. Conceit however, manifests itself negatively as an audible and excessive expression of self-esteem. Strangely enough, it is often an indication of insecurity. Human beings who carry a good deal of fear in social situations will sometimes react with an air of defensiveness. They will become aloof and look over the heads of other people, rather than into their eyes. To a casual observer, it will appear that they do not care about the other people in the room and that they are snobbish and stuck-up. They will appear to be *conceited*, but in fact they are simply afraid. This is also another indication of a lack of social awareness. People who understand the social graces of getting along with people will make an effort to look other people in the eye and speak with anyone who approaches them, regardless of any fear that they may feel. People who exhibit conceit because of insecurity fail on a lot of levels.

All conceit is not the result of fear. Some folks actually believe that they are better than the average human being. They have such a narcissistic, self love of themselves that they are unable to bring themselves out of the stratosphere and down to earth with the rest of us. They believe that their status, their wealth, their intelligence, or perhaps their heritage has placed them on a higher evolutionary plain than the majority of the population. What they fail to notice is that most people on the planet find them offensive. They are the vain, self-important, snobs of the world. They have incredibly low social awareness and they are often very unhappy. You only have to look at the alarming number of suicides and drug overdoses amongst movie stars, music idols, and socialites to know that it is not only lonely at the top…it is also a very sad place to be. Narcissistic people tend to be so out of touch with social awareness that they have trouble navigating in society at all. They are lost souls. Often, drugs and suicide attempts are the tragic vehicles they utilize to bring themselves back to reality or completely out of it into the safety and solitude of the afterlife.

My way of dealing with conceited people is to treat them like anyone else. I don't attempt to emulate them and I don't try to live up to their standards or values. I do not envy what they have and I do not take anything they say personally. I listen to what they have to say and I express the same level of interest in their conversation as I would with anyone else. If they say something that I do not understand, I ask them to explain it to me. I am not afraid to show vulnerability to them but I also refuse to show any fear or idolatry toward them. If their conceit is based in insecurity, they usually enjoy my candid approach. They want a normal relationship with a normal, respectful human being just like anyone else. If their conceit is based in narcissism, they tend to be taken aback but intrigued none-the-less. In other words, because conceited people are used to having people sucking-up to them, when they find themselves being treated like normal human beings, they often enjoy the exchange. I will admit that some conceited people are so self-absorbed that it is impossible to have a normal relationship with them, but I have found that most of them are approachable if I just act like myself. Generally, if you try to be someone you are not, you will fail to get along with other people. That applies to conceited people just as it does with anyone else, so don't try to be like them and don't pretend to understand what their life is like. Avoid the tendency to treat them like the superior humans they think they are and do not allow them to subjugate you with their high and mighty behavior. Be yourself and your natural essence will prevail.

Remember that conceit is negative and that it should not be allowed to breathe. Do not feed it with acceptance of narcissistic behavior and do not fuel it by sucking-up to vanity or arrogance. If you can summon up enough courage to challenge the lair of the dragon of conceit, and the dragon is willing to listen, tell him how you feel and boldly state that his behavior is unacceptable in civilized society. You might not stop him, but you might just slow him down a little. Conceited people don't appreciate being observed in anything less than a glowing blaze of light. If they are cognizant of the fact that the people around them think less of them because of their behavior, they might change in order to put themselves back on their self-indulgent pedestal. Conceited people are extremely difficult to get along with and trying is often unrewarding. However, it is possible to break through to many of them with good old-fashioned reason and common sense. Give it a try. You have nothing to lose, (except a bad relationship) and everything to gain.

LIARS

LIARS are very difficult to get along with…and why would anyone want to get along with them anyway? As mentioned earlier, most people have exaggerated a story or told a white lie from time to time. The liars we are talking about here are those compulsive liars who lie so often that it is impossible to know when they are telling the truth. They become so accustomed to lying that they see nothing wrong with it. It is how they get through life. So why do they do it?

People who often choose lies over the truth are generally insecure and deeply dishonest. They have decided that because of past negative events in their lives, the truth is likely to cause them hardship or heartbreak. Those negative events have driven them to a life of insecurity and constant fear that their inadequacies will be discovered and laid out for the world to see. They believe that their lies protect them. Their exaggerated untruths make them feel safe. They think that they are much better off for having said something that makes them appear to be more important than they are or hides the real truth. In some cases, they are so attached to the world of untruth that they are actually able to convince themselves that their lies are in fact, the truth or that no one else in the world has any idea that they are lying. Their entire life becomes a lie and they will fight to the death to maintain their right to lie in any situation. These people live among us. They are clerks, accountants, company presidents, equipment operators and bankers. Think about the folks at the much berated Enron Corporation. Highly sophisticated business people at Enron, who could easily have made millions of dollars with simple honesty, told huge lies every day in order to better their positions. Those Enron guys were not unique or special. The world is full of liars and cheats in all walks of life, in many families, and in all socio-economic groups.

The best way to deal with a compulsive liar or even someone who has lied to you only once or twice is to confront him on his most recent lie. Make sure you have your facts straight and then hit him between the eyes, (gently) with it. As is the case in most confrontations it is best to speak of only one issue at a time, so don't blurt out a litany of potential lying crimes that you think he may have committed. Find out exactly what the truth is and tell him in private that you have evidence that he may be wrong. Lay out what you know and allow him to respond. Do not accuse him of lying at the outset. Instead, ask him why his information is dramatically different than what you believe to be true. The object is to get him talking about the facts of the lie so that he has an opportunity to think, rather than going on the defensive immediately. Maintain your composure and wait for him to explain himself. Stick to your guns but do not become angry, abrasive or sarcastic. Any of those reactions will put up a wall that will end any chance you have of improving the behavior. Remember that you want to get along with the liar. You cannot create a good relationship with him in the future if you berate and emotionally destroy him today. Whether he admits to his lie or not, make it very clear to him that you do not appreciate being lied to and that you will not tolerate it now or in the future. Let him know that going forward, you will expect the full and complete truth at all times. That is the only effective way to create an environment of trust with someone who lies to you.

If you don't confront a liar, he will simply continue to lie. He will assume he is getting away with it. Even if he suspects that you know he is lying, if you don't object, he will continue to do it because it carries no consequences. As tough as it may seem, you will be doing yourself and the liar a favor by confronting him and asking him to stop. Frankly, if he can't stop lying, despite your best efforts to rehabilitate him, you will probably never be able to get along with him. Not getting along with a compulsive, unrepentant liar may be the best thing for all concerned. However, if you are able to rehabilitate a liar through proactive, kind confrontation, you will have made a difference that will improve his life immeasurably.

PREDJUDICED PEOPLE

PREDJUDICED PEOPLE are perhaps some of the most objectionable people in western society. North America has been a haven for people of various cultures from many countries for hundreds of years. We proudly recognize our cultural diversity and use the term *melting pot of humanity* as a badge of honor. And yet, we still find a huge number of people here who have problems with other people because of race, creed, color, gender, religion, sexual orientation, and a hodge-podge of other unavoidable conditions. Other words for prejudice include *chauvinism, narrow mindedness, discrimination, bigotry, bias, and intolerance.* My dictionary defines prejudice as: *An unfavorable opinion or feeling formed beforehand or without knowledge, thought or reason.* There are other definitions, but that one is the best description of it that I could find. Clearly the people who write dictionaries feel that prejudice is the result of empty-headedness. I tend to agree. It seems to me that the folks in the *melting pot* are not melting at the same rate and are instead bobbing around in the pot, bumping heads with each other.

The synonyms shown in the foregoing paragraph along with the definition clearly and simply tell us what prejudice is. But what causes it? My opinion is that it is often based in fear. Referring back to our old nemesis, Adolf Hitler, it is clear that the Nazi holocaust was driven by fear of the Jewish culture in Europe. Folks of Jewish extraction were, (and still are) generally very intelligent and at the time, many of them were successful business people. They controlled a lot of the fiscal wealth in Europe, which caused Hitler and his gang to fear their influence and their potential to control the destiny of his country. In Hitler's crazed mind, rounding them up and killing them was the best course of action. The holocaust was perhaps, the worst case of racial prejudice in the history of the world. In the new millennium civilized cultures kill fewer people, en masse because of their racial background, but it is possible that there is more race-based hate on our planet than ever before.

Prejudiced people, or bigots as they are often known, are easy to identify. You know the type: ignorant boors who refuse to listen to any commentary that supports anything they do not believe in. My dictionary defines bigots as: *people who are utterly intolerant of any creed, belief, or race that is not their own.* My goodness, they certainly must have a self-limiting existence! Not only must they stay within their own neighborhoods and associate only with people that are like them, (other bigots) but they must limit their thoughts to total negativity toward all people except themselves and their flock of bigots. You can expect the bigots you meet to make salacious, insulting commentary about almost any minority, religion or culture other than their own. In most cases, they will have grown up in an environment that supported and encouraged bigoted intolerance as a normal way of life. They believe their way is the only way and anyone who disagrees with them does not deserve a place on their planet. At the very least, they believe that minorities and those with opposing beliefs should be isolated and forced to live somewhere else. For bigots, bigotry is righteous and good. Interestingly, they don't actually know that they are bigots. They think they are normal and everyone else is warped. At this point, I am sure you are wondering what kind of advice I can possibly give you to make getting along with bigots easier! Frankly, so am I!

Fortunately, the world is evolving and to some extent, bigots are evolving out of it. Generation Y, the largest generation of our times, has a much smaller percentage of intolerant people in it than Generation X and the Boomers had before them. Society is attempting to cleanse itself and with luck and diligence, perhaps our world will get back on the path it tried to start with the Ten Commandments. In the meantime, unless you want to become a bigot yourself, your only chance for getting along with people with extreme prejudice is to show them the error of their ways. Just as you would with a liar, avoid confronting or embarrassing a bigot publicly and do not challenge him with anger, or sarcasm. Be patient and understand that he is not really aware of the error of his ways. If you challenge a bigot, you run the risk of becoming the target of his venom. You might end up joining the ranks of those he hates and at that point you will have lost any chance of helping him. When you do talk to him, discuss the reasons why his point of view is different than yours and gently move him toward the path of tolerating others. Tell him about the value that each person brings to the world and state specific facts that support your views. The chances are that he will know exactly what you are talking about the minute you start talking. Bigots are not necessarily lacking in intelligence, they simply have a socially unacceptable view of how the world should work. They are not completely without empathy…they have empathy for those they accept. However, they have no empathy whatsoever for the group or groups of people that they choose not to tolerate.

In the majority of cases, bigots cannot change their thinking completely. The fear and intolerance that drives them is often so ingrained that it can never be erased. The best you can hope for is that they keep their intolerance to themselves and refrain from publicly insulting or harming members of their target groups. If you can convince them to keep their venom inside, you will have improved the world just a little, and you might find that they have a good deal of value in many areas. It is possible that they can be a positive force in your life and in the lives of others. Do not allow that one area of weakness in their psyche to eliminate everything good they might have to offer. Do not hate them because they hate others. That would simply put you on the same level as them. Oh and by the way, some people think that bigoted humor is simply *humor*. Jokes about other races and religions are common in our society. They are not appropriate, but they are common nonetheless. If you fail to see the humor in them, do not make the mistake of exhibiting self-righteous indignation when in the presence of it. That will only make your behavior the cause for a passive-aggressive attack against you by the offenders. Instead, accept the humor for what it is but slowly and deliberately attempt to convince the individuals involved to amend their use of it. There are lots of funny things in the world. Insulting and embarrassing other human beings is not one of them. However, you can do nothing about it if you become excommunicated from the people responsible for it.

Getting along with prejudiced people is not easy but if you can change the heart and soul of one bigot for the better, your life will be enriched.

SARCASTIC PEOPLE

SARCASTIC PEOPLE are oh, so annoying! You know who I am talking about: Those silly, insulting smart-asses that inhabit almost every working group, business club, and family on earth. Sarcasm is a strictly human trait. I am certain that scientists have not been able to identify any similar characteristic amongst wolves, birds or fish. So why, you might ask would human beings see the need to adopt such a clearly insulting and unnecessary behavior?

Here is what one dictionary says about sarcasm: *1. Harsh or bitter derision or irony. 2. A sharply ironical taunt or gibe; a sneering or cutting remark.*

My thesaurus offers the following synonyms: *irony, mockery, derision, scorn, disdain, cynicism.*

The next time you decide to make a sarcastic remark, think about what you just read. Do you really want to be the sarcastic person described in these definitions? A lot of people think that sarcasm is cute or funny, when in fact by definition it is intended to be hurtful. Its singular purpose is to put another person down and often it is used to win an argument or put the sarcastic person into a position of power. It is the weapon of small minds and weak hearts. It is the final volley by people who have long since run out of meaningful arguments. It is used to demean and disarm a person of integrity by a person whose integrity has taken flight.

Sarcasm is often a fear response. When a person has run out of good and reasonable ideas, they might resort to sarcasm to weaken the other person's position. Typically when they feel that they are losing an argument or that their own position is weak, they will resort to sarcastic mockery during which they will use words that say the opposite of what they really mean. The mockery is often accompanied by a change in tonal inflection, which will sound demeaning all on its own.

In some cases people can become so attached to sarcasm that they utilize it even when there is nothing for them to gain by it. These are the perennial smart-asses that pop into our lives from time to time. With luck and effort we are able to pop them back out of our lives or change their attitude before they drive us crazy. If you know someone who is a sarcastic smart-ass, understand that there is probably some underlying insecurity that she is attempting to hide by putting the limelight onto others with her remarks. A person who mocks people or makes ironical insults toward others on a regular basis may have spent a good deal of time defending herself from others while in her formative years. Alternatively, she may in fact have a very high opinion of herself, (see: conceited people) such that she believes by putting other people down she makes herself look better. In that case, you may be dealing with a person with deeply rooted narcissism. That person might have spent her formative years being constantly praised and positively compared to other children. She might have been what is commonly referred to as a *spoiled brat*. Even in adulthood her need to always be the centre of attention may cause her to diminish the value of all but a few people in her life. A person with that much self-love will probably exhibit other forms of anti-social behavior as well. Sarcasm may be only one of the many weapons she uses to hurt others.

When I am confronted with sarcasm, I must admit that it is all I can do to prevent myself from responding in kind. Usually, the hair on the back of my neck will begin to rise and my primeval desire to fight back will race to the surface. In the past, I would often let my emotions take over and start the fight. Sometimes I would respond with my own sarcastic remark and other times I would simply offer an angry, negative retort. That generally ended any hope for an intelligent conclusion to whatever discussion I was having. In essence the sarcastic person won as soon as I lost my composure. Now, when faced with sarcasm, I tend to take a deep breath and compose myself before I speak at all. Once I have processed the comment and decided to deal with it, I can calmly move the conversation in a more intelligent direction.

The best way to deal with sarcasm is to calmly ask the individual if they are serious. In some cases, sarcasm is intended to be genuinely humorous so it is best to ask the intention of the sarcastic person before reacting to it. If they intended humor they will admit to it and you can move on. If they are genuinely trying to harm you in some way or beat you at something, the question will force them to move back to the original discussion. They will know that they have been caught in the act and will be forced to deal with the original topic in a serious and straightforward manner. After you have completed the discussion you should recall the sarcastic remark and let them know that it did not aid the discussion. If the sarcasm is habitual or chronic, you will do yourself and the sarcastic person a favor by pointing out to her that it is not acceptable and that she would do well to modify her attitude. With any luck she will thank you. At the very least, she will be much more concerned about her verbal attacks in the future.

Getting along with sarcastic people is not easy, but there are worse things and from my perspective, sarcasm is not something that should be allowed to seriously harm a relationship.

KNOW-IT-ALLS

KNOW-IT-ALLS are interesting people. These are the guys and gals who have an answer for everything and know more about everything in the universe than anyone else. They can't wait to tell you that you are wrong and they love to let you have their expert opinion on just about anything you might mention. Let's not forget that annoying trait of *one-upping* everyone. No matter what you might have done, they have done more of it, or theirs is bigger and better.

The hyphenated word, *"know-it-all"* is actually, and surprisingly, in my dictionary. It is defined as: *Somebody claiming to know everything.* The synonyms in my thesaurus are: *egghead, bighead,* and *clever person.*

I am not sure I agree with the list of synonyms since know-it-alls are often not clever at all. Sometimes they actually seem quite dim and the *"everything"* that they claim to know is often simplistic or actually wrong! These folks are shameless blowhards who feel the need to overpower everyone around them with their self-proclaimed superiority. Know-it-alls have an incredible lack of social awareness that prevents them from recognizing the negative reactions they may be receiving from others due to their braggadocios behavior. They also possess a significantly diminished lack of self-awareness that prevents them from understanding that there is something fundamentally wrong with the obnoxious way they present themselves. Know-it-alls like to be the centre of attention. Their egocentric behavior is likely the result of deeply seated insecurity that causes them to seek attention or alternatively, a feeling of superiority over all others.

You must be careful when expounding on any subject unless you have already proven yourself to be an expert. If you know a little about everything, as many *trivia experts* do, you must be cautious about the attitude you project when you are involved in discussions. If you present an air of superiority while giving folks the benefit of your wealth of knowledge, you might be branded a know-it-all.

Getting along with know-it-alls requires patience and kindness. They think they can impress you with their knowledge while creating a persona of importance and intellect for themselves. If you decide to go *toe to toe* with them and argue against one of their ideas, you must make sure you have proof of your convictions at hand. They will argue to the death unless you have irrefutable proof of their wrongness. Even if you have irrefutable proof, some of the more unrepentant know-it-alls will refuse to accept it; preferring instead to stubbornly remain true to their own incorrect beliefs. Their stubbornness might infuriate you to the point that you want to yell at them or resort to physical violence. In many cases you might simply choose to avoid them in the future. A negative or confrontational reaction will not help you get along with a know-it-all.

Like all folks with personality quirks, know-it-alls do not want to be publicly embarrassed because of their shortcomings. If you want to improve their behavior so that you can get along with them, you need to have a quiet one-on-one discussion, out of earshot of anyone else. Tell him that you like him, (or love him if that is the case) and then let him know that his constant barrage of trivia and bragging makes him sound like a know-it-all. His reaction will probably be defensive, but stand firm and give some specific examples to reinforce your point of view. At that point you should tell him about all of his good and wonderful qualities and that it is only this one thing that is holding him back from a better relationship with you. Even if he doesn't agree at that moment that he is, in fact a know-it-all, he will have it on his mind from that day forward and his behavior is likely to improve.

EVERYONE HAS AN EGO

EVERYONE you meet is likely to do or say something that offends or annoys you from time to time. In all cases, it is best to sit back, take a deep breath, and avoid an emotional reaction. Think about what occurred and make a value judgment of just how badly the act or comment has harmed you before you do or say anything.

Remember that arguments are a result of ego. Egoism is a dangerous but unavoidable human trait. One dictionary definition for Egoism is: *the habit of valuing everything only in reference to one's personal interests.* Synonyms are: *selfishness, self-centeredness, insensitivity,* and *lack of concern for others.* The opposite of egoism is altruism, which has synonyms that include: *selflessness, unselfishness, humanity* and *philanthropy.* Altruists have a much better chance of getting along with people than egoists ever will. By the way, egoism is not to be confused with *egotism,* which is defined as: *excessive and objectionable reference to oneself in conversation or writing.* For a better understanding of egotism, read the previous section on conceited people again. It occurs to me that egotistical people probably stopped reading this book a long time ago because none of the concepts in it matter to them.

When faced with an annoying person, remove your ego from your thought process and try to evaluate the encounter based on its specific merits. For example, when you are in the presence of a conceited person, ask yourself if her conceit can actually harm you in any way. After all, she is really only harming her own reputation and it is not your responsibility to *fix* her. When insulted by a sarcastic person, try not to take his sarcasm personally and accept the fact that he forces his bad behavior on everyone…it is not all about you! If you have the confidence and courage to put your ego on the shelf, it will be much easier to decide on a course of action that will create a positive result. Ego-based, emotional responses to negative situations almost always create an even more negative result. Your ego quite naturally tells you that no one has the right to insult you or attack you in any way so you must work very hard to repress it.

Ego forms a very large part of the competitive nature of human beings. It is what makes the human race special and it is safe to say that without ego, we would not have become the supreme beings on our planet. It is what makes us learn and invent things. It is what drives us to make money and find cures for diseases. It is what led our forefathers to find North America and it is what drove modern man into outer space. Ego is also, unfortunately, what has led us into war, time and time again, and it is responsible for a lot of the problems we have on planet earth today.

People without any ego at all are either mentally disturbed or dead. However, if you want to get along with people and allow every person you meet to become a positive force in your life you must learn to control your ego and try to avoid the temptation to turn every situation into a personal victory. Accept the fact that when you defend yourself or *fight back* you are in fact, fighting. Your retaliatory words and actions will start a war that you cannot win. Opposing armies in a war never get along with each other until several people have been harmed. If you allow your ego to lose the first battle while making the decision to work on a peace treaty, ultimate victory will be yours.

The wonderful contradiction in all of this is that allowing one's ego to take a beating in order to get along with difficult people is very good for one's ego! The high road is a lonely but extremely gratifying road, indeed.

What did we learn in Chapter Ten?

- Before you can deal with a rude person you must understand why they choose to be rude.

- Treat conceited people just like anyone else.

- Liars must be confronted with their lies.

- Bigotry is a result of fear and social environment.

- Sarcasm should not be returned.

- Know-it-alls may feel insecure or even superior to others.

- Ego is the reason for most disagreements.

TEN "EASY" COMMANDMENTS FOR GETTING ALONG WITH PEOPLE.

"If you want to get along with people, give them lots of reasons to get along with you."

CHAPTER 11

In this final chapter, I want to focus in on *you*. If you want to improve your ability to have positive relationships with others, the first person to work on is *you*. Knowing what makes other people difficult to get along with is only part of the puzzle. If you don't understand and recognize your own behavioral traits, you will get nowhere with others. Here are my ten "EASY" commandments for getting along with people:

FIRST COMMANDMENT
TAKE RESPONSIBILITY FOR EVERYTHING YOU DO

You must first remember that the most important person in any relationship is you. That is because the only person you can truly control is you. You are totally responsible for everything you do, and you have no choice but to live with the consequences of your own words and actions. Your life is made up of the choices you make.

Remember that you are just as responsible for your failures as your successes. Isn't it interesting though, that most people will raise a joyful ruckus and take complete credit for something that goes well for them, but when something goes wrong, they immediately begin to play the blame-game? It is a natural human trait to look for someone else to blame when things go wrong. *"I divorced him because he didn't understand me." "I haven't had a raise in years because my boss doesn't like me." "I didn't pass the test because they didn't give me enough time to study." "I don't have any money because the Government takes it all for taxes." "It doesn't matter how hard I try, she never praises me."* If these statements sound familiar it is because you can identify with them. You will hear someone in your life making statements like this every day of your life. These are examples of statements that human beings make in order to avoid or deflect blame and responsibility for their own disappointments.

People find all kinds of ways to avoid responsibility. How many times have you heard people blaming *something* when things go wrong? *"I couldn't get it done because I just didn't have the time." "My life sucks because all I ever do is work." "I hate my job but I can't quit because I love the people here." "We wanted to have more children but we just couldn't afford it."* In each of these cases, there is someone else in exactly the same situation and from the same socio-economic background that will get things done on time, enjoy life despite their work, quit their job for one they like, or have all the children they want. The difference is as simple as choices. People who get what they want out of life take responsibility for everything they do and make positive choices to take them where they want to go.

When you point out to someone who does not take responsibility for her life that someone else is doing some or all of the things that she cannot get done, she will often answer with something like, *"I just don't know how he does it!" "They can't possibly afford that!"* or *"Eventually it will all catch up with her!"* The tendency seems to be to put doubt in other people's minds that taking responsibility and getting what we want out of life through positive effort carries negative connotations. Of course the reasons for this phenomenon are based in insecurity and defensiveness. The person, who is holding herself back because she is afraid to take a chance, wants to make it appear that the person who chose to move forward is making a huge mistake. She feels that if she criticizes the positive, proactive person, her own lack of success will go unnoticed or become somehow more acceptable. If she chose to think fewer negative thoughts and replaced them with positive thoughts, her life would move in a positive, successful direction. Negativity is easier than positivity. Negativity can be done while sitting down. When you choose to move your life in a positive direction however, you have to stand up and *do something*. People who are branded as *lazy* have usually chosen negativity. People who are branded as *industrious* or *successful* have chosen positivity. Which would you rather be?

While the negative people are blaming others and finding fault with successful people for their efforts, they are not getting along with very many people. They have chosen a path that will not allow good relationships to exist. Instead they are attempting to tear down the good that positive, responsible people are valiantly trying to build. Usually they will not admit, or perhaps are not cognizant of the fact that their efforts only serve to harm their more industrious counterparts. Usually, only other negative people will want to associate with them. However, because negativity is easy, it can be somewhat contagious and negative people are always looking for new recruits. Be on guard for negative people and do not make the mistake of being dragged into their web of deceit and sadness.

Once you have mastered taking responsibility for yourself and living positively, you still have a lot to consider if you want to give every person the opportunity to become a positive force in your life. If you want to get along with people you have to give them reasons to get along with you. You need to become a person that everyone looks up to at all times, and in all circumstances.

SECOND COMMANDMENT
APOLOGIZE SINCERELY

When was the last time you said you were sorry…and meant it? The words, *"I am sorry,"* are used quite routinely as a way of getting past uncomfortable situations. Often an apology is not sincere at all. It is merely a convenient way to prevent another person from retaliating against a person who has done something wrong. Once you have said the magic words, "I am sorry," you feel that you are off the hook and all is well with the world. The person who was wronged however, may be left with a disturbing doubt that your apology might not have been genuine and that you are only pandering to his or her injured pride. Frankly, if your apology is not sincere, the other person will know it. Your body language and your tone of voice will give you away.

Scientifically, human communication is made up of 3 elements. In 1971, Albert Mehrabian published a study of communication that later came to be known as the *three V's*. They are: *Verbal, Vocal and Visual*. The first V, verbal, represents the spoken word and it represents only 7% of communication. The second V, vocal, represents tone of voice and it represents 38% of communication. The third V, visual, represents body language or totally non-verbal communication and it represents a whopping 55% of all communication. That being the case, the verbalized words, "I am sorry" will only have meaningful impact if your vocal and visual presentations indicate sincerity. A sarcastic tone or a failure to make eye contact will tip the person off every time. If you are not actually sorry for whatever you did or said to upset another person, before you apologize, think the situation over and determine why you are not feeling remorse. Discuss the situation with the other person and then offer a sincere, heartfelt apology. Once your apology has been accepted, do everything you can to make things right. Always remember that an insincere apology is worse than no apology at all, so don't resort to the comment, *"Well I said I was sorry, didn't I???"* to dominate a conversation. Insincerity will nullify any apology, rendering it worthless.

Apologies are not unlike true gratitude. Not everyone is in the habit of using apologies as, and when they should. Some people stubbornly refuse to say they are sorry for something they have done. Many folks do not understand when an apology is in order and some have a great fear of showing vulnerability. The most objectionable members of mankind are simply so aloof and have such huge feelings of superiority that they do not see the need to offer apologies to other human beings for virtually any wrong they commit.

If you want to get along with people, apologize when you know that you are wrong. Apologies don't hurt anyone and they are a great way to show off your integrity and courage. Once you accept the fact that making mistakes, saying offensive things, and being wrong are all part of being human you will find apologizing much easier. Try it…you will like it… and so will everyone around you!

THIRD COMMANDMENT
EXERCISE PATIENCE

If you want to get along with people, you must be patient. It is a fact that when people put you out of your comfort zone you are likely to become impatient. For example, if you are a hard working, *let's-get-it-done* kind of person and you are attempting to build a sundeck with a slow moving, *let's-take-our-time* neighbor you are likely to find his work habits unacceptable. While you are trying to speed things up, he will be trying to slow you down. He might complain about the pace you are trying to work at and he might want to take several breaks, while you just want to keep working. Your natural, human response to this situation is to become impatient, annoyed and ultimately, angry. When you finally lose your patience, you will immediately stop getting along with him. Your body language will show your frustration and your verbalization may either become loud and demanding or cool and quiet. Either way, he will know that you are annoyed with him. You will have set the scene for a war and the only way you can avoid it is to walk away. Once you have walked away, your neighbor will probably begin talking about you behind your back to his friends and family and you might do the same to him. You might be able to repair the damage, reconcile, and resume your friendship or you might end the relationship forever. No matter how it turns out, damage has been done and time has been lost…all because you were impatient.

Be careful in expressing frustration or perplexed amazement when someone in your life does not understand what you are saying or answers in a fashion you do not approve of. Some of the people in my life will occasionally seem quite disgusted with me if I forget a date or simply cannot remember someone's name. If I forget something that happened twenty years ago that is extremely important to them, they seem to feel that I am either lying about my lack of memory of the event, or that I am an insensitive lout for having no memory of it. Their impatience in these situations is palpable and it usually results in embarrassment or frustration for me. At that point, I am inclined to end the conversation, or sometimes I will spend the next several minutes chatting mindlessly about it in order to jog my memory and restore my credibility. In some cases anger will take over and a war will break out. Impatience during conversations is all too common and it prevents good and effective communication. If someone is having trouble understanding you or remembering what you are talking about, help him instead of showing impatience. Your relationships will improve immeasurably if you remember just that one thing.

Patience means slowing down and allowing yourself to accept people the way they are. If you choose to associate with someone who works slower than you, accept that they will not speed up to meet your standards. If you have a desire to make millions of dollars and you work with someone who is happy being in the moderately paid middle class, accept that not everyone wants to be rich. If you fall in love with a girl who is religious, and you are not, you should accept that her view of the world and her way of functioning in it is probably going to be much different than yours. People tend to believe that other people should live by their perceptions and their standards. When they come across folks who have opposing viewpoints, they become frustrated and immediately go about trying to *fix* them. When your impatience causes you to try to *fix* another person to make them more like you, it usually does not end well. Your view of the world is not the *only* view and your insistence in forcing your own agenda is frustrating and hurtful to others. Remember the old adage: *"Patience is a virtue."* I agree with that completely and I try not to lose my patience with anyone everyday.

FOURTH COMMANDMENT
ALWAYS SHOW GRATITUDE

Do you show your gratitude to others for what you receive everyday? If you don't, you are missing out on a multitude of opportunities for happiness. The dictionary defines gratitude simply as: *"a feeling of being thankful to somebody for doing something."* Synonyms are: *thankfulness* and *appreciation*. Do you consistently show the people in your life that you appreciate the things they do that impact on your life in the smallest or greatest of ways? It is extremely easy to say, *"I truly appreciate everything you have done for me."* Easier yet is, *"Great job."* The easiest thing of all to say is, *"Thanks!"* Why not say one or all of those things regularly?

Sadly, many people are so stiff and afraid of removing their security armor that they will only offer tangible gratitude when prodded by another person or when forced by a need for political correctness. When they finally offer gratitude or a simple *thank you,* it comes across as stilted or phony. If you want to be appreciated by more people, drop your guard and embrace your vulnerability. Folks who always recognize the positive efforts of others are universally admired and adored. Don't be one of those unappreciative people. When you know that someone has done something for you that they did not have to do...thank them! If someone goes above and beyond for you and creates something good that improves your life, remember to show your appreciation in any small, but meaningful way. Give them a flower, send them a card, say thank you...*DO SOMETHING!*

In order to show gratitude that matters, you must actually mean it and believe in it yourself. There is nothing worse than fake gratitude. That phenomenon can come about in one of two ways: when you say thanks to someone because you feel it is the politically correct thing to do or when you are really not thankful at all for what has been done. If you don't believe it, don't say it. Saying thank you when you do not mean it will do more harm than good. If you find yourself in a situation where you either do not appreciate what someone has done for you or you have other outstanding issues with him, explain what has created your negative feelings. Hopefully you can come to a meeting of the minds and at the end of the conversation you will be able to thank him for his kindness with conviction. Gratitude comes from pure appreciation along with the ability to simultaneously exhibit vulnerability and courage. Some people want to say *thanks* but because of their own insecurity, simply cannot. Others are so insensitive or aloof that they do not see the need for a display of gratitude. One is just as bad as the other.

Everyone you meet has an ego that needs stroking despite how humble or unassuming they might seem. They expect to be acknowledged for the good things they do and they will shower the people who understand and recognize them for their good deeds with appreciation in return. Great people spend their entire lives doing good things for others and thriving on the gratitude they receive. If you want to get along with more people than you do now, always genuinely and respectfully show appreciation for every good thing that happens to you. Don't forget to say, *"Thank you, Thank you, Thank you!"* How hard is that?

FIFTH COMMANDMENT
BRING HUMOR TO EVERY RELATIONSHIP

One of the surest ways to get along with people is to make them laugh. It is no accident that some of the most idolized and wealthy people in the world started out as comedians. People who have an ability to make other people laugh have a talent that is worth its weight in gold. Humor is the fastest route to the hearts of everyone on earth and I am a huge believer in its value to society. People who are serious all the time are dull and forgettable. Funny people who smile and laugh a lot, on the other hand, are lovable and memorable. Their manner is attractive to others and their joy of life is infectious. Any shortcomings of a funny person are easily overlooked and forgiven because of their good nature.

When in grade school, as a smaller child who did not like to fight, I discovered that the tough guys in my school could be charmed with humor. *(Fortunately, I began my study of human nature at an early age and it kept me out of harms way on many occasions.)* I realized after a bit of trial and error that even the bullies in my school wanted to hang out with someone who would make them laugh. When challenged by a bully I would deflect his threats with compliments and then summon up all of the funny commentary I could in order to put a smile on his face and take the focus off of my impending beating. In no time, I would have him laughing and in all but the most incorrigible cases, I was able to turn a bully into a friend with nary a scratch to my delicate body. They never knew what hit them. Despite their need to exercise their natural animalistic tendencies to take advantage of a weaker prey, they could not help but put their need for dominance aside when faced with the power of smiles and chuckles. The best thing about my technique with bullies was that when they realized that I could make them laugh, they tended to want to look after me and keep me safe. I went from elementary school to high school graduation without ever being in any sort of serious fight because my bully-buddies always stepped in when anyone so much as looked at me the wrong way. Humor will make the meanest men laugh, the saddest men smile and the happiest men weep with joy. It has more followers than any politician and greater curative powers than any antibiotic.

I was also a *class-clown* in school, which got me past the wrath of many-a-teacher. At some point I came to the realization that if someone was laughing at me, it was almost impossible for him or her to become angry with me. Whenever I sensed that I was about to get into trouble I would summon up the most appropriate humor I could under the circumstances to take the focus off my bad behavior or lousy test scores. In most cases I was able to put a smile on the teacher's face and avoid a lecture or a detention. That worked quite well until parent-teacher nights when invariably, teachers would tell my folks that even though I was a joy to have in class, I was not applying myself and could surely do better. Whenever that happened *the jig was up* because my parents knew me too well to be swayed by a joke or a smile from their unscholarly son. Even though I received no points for humor on my report cards, I learned to survive in society with a smile, a laugh, and a twinkle in my eye. I have used that skill to carry me all the way to this stage of my life. I have learned some other skills along the way, but I truly believe that my sense of humor has been largely responsible for whatever opportunities and successes life has blessed me with so far.

I suppose you can get through life without a sense of humor, but why would you want to? Laughing is healthy. Here are some facts that scientifically support my love of humor: Laughter lowers blood pressure by causing deeper breathing and increased oxygenation to the blood stream. Laughter decreases stress hormones and increases infection-fighting antibodies. Regular laughter is good for the heart because it increases heart rate and pulse. Laughter is a good workout for your diaphragm, abdominal muscles, respiratory system, and back muscles. Laughter can benefit digestion and burn calories. Laughter stimulates both sides of the brain to enhance learning and reduce psychological stress, which allows easier learning and better information retention. It also increases overall alertness. In short, humor can provide you with a longer, healthier life. The great bonus is that your mental, emotional and intellectual health will be greatly enhanced. And let's not forget that humor and laughter are fun!

Laughter may be the best way of all to improve and maintain relationships. It brings people together and seldom tears them apart. Most humor is positive and even bad humor is forgivable. When things get rough and life is lagging, humor is invaluable in making things seem better. People would much rather associate with a funny person than a sad, depressed, angry, or boring one. If you want to have more good relationships in your life, work on your sense of humor and exercise it regularly with everyone you meet.

<u>SIXTH COMMANDMENT</u>
LISTEN WELL

Do you listen? Do you really listen? Or do you just listen until you hear something you disagree with? Listening has to do with a lot more than the ability to hear and understand auditory signals from other humans. Listening has to do with *caring* about what the other person is saying. In times past, on many occasions, I found myself listening briefly, hearing something that I did not agree with, and then mentally tuning out for the next several minutes. From that point forward I was like *Charlie Brown* in the *Peanuts* comic strip who only heard, *"whah, whah, whah,"* from the people that spoke to him. At some point, when I felt it was my turn to speak, I would rail on about the one thing that I did not agree with. I would neither hear nor feel what my conversation partners were trying to convey to me. I did not care about their feelings or what the deeper meaning of their commentary might have been. Although I had heard, I had not listened. Although I was aware of what they had said, I had not grasped the importance of it to *them*. My competitive nature and my desire to set them straight on the one thing that was important to me would lead me to an insensitive and self-centered response.

You have probably read or heard a thousand times that you need to be *present* for other people. That means that you must be alert, aware, and focused on the people you communicate with. You cannot have a meaningful conversation with someone while you are playing a video game or watching television. When you make the conscious decision to speak with another human being, you must clear your mind of all extraneous thoughts, put aside any distractions, and focus on the person in front of you. Only when your singular interest is the person in front of you can you truly listen to them. Once you are fully focused, listen very closely to what they are saying and try to read between the lines if their meaning is not clear. Successful people are almost always exceptional listeners. Genuine listening is the secret to your success as a friend, wife, husband, leader, teammate, manager or colleague.

SEVENTH COMMANDMENT
DON'T BE A WHINER

I love to spend time with people who don't complain. I like them so much that if I had to choose to eliminate one sort of person from earth, I would probably choose the whining complainers of the world. Those folks can generally find something negative in any situation, and they manage to boil every one of them down to something that affects them personally. A whiner will think that the rising cost of gasoline affects him more than anyone else. He will also believe that no one else can understand how he feels about the cost of gasoline because he is *different* and his situation is more challenging. He lives in a *woe is me* world where in his mind, he is victimized daily while everyone else lives a life of pampered privilege.

As an operations manager who had to oversee many managers, I always found that each manager felt her office and her situation was *different*. When a more positive manager would express optimism and positive thinking about her position as a manager, other managers would become quite annoyed, stating that their offices were different and their problems were greater. In fact, in most cases the positive managers had tougher offices to run and their jobs were much more challenging than those of their negative counterparts. Complainers see the world as a place that is out to get them. In order to keep the world from hurting him or her, they are always on the attack… challenging every person and organization with whining before they can be accused of failure. When they know that failure is imminent, they begin to whine and moan to fend off the blows of truth. They believe that whining and moaning will protect them from failure and deflect attention away from it. In reality, a whiner's grim protestations only serve to make him seem trite and annoying to everyone around him.

If you want to get along with people, don't whine and complain. My thesaurus gives the following synonyms for the word, whiner: *grumbler, grouch, complainer, wailer, objector*, and *protester*. Are you any of those? Do you want to be thought of as any of those? Probably not! However, a sizable number of you reading this book are guilty of whining and complaining from time to time. A smaller, but still sizable number of you whine and complain on a regular basis. I have two words for you: Stop it!

When someone else gets an award and you are overlooked, don't complain…go out and do something to earn your own award. When you find out that someone makes more money than you, don't whine…

work harder or go out and get a better job so that you can make more money than they do. When you can't afford to buy a new car, don't whine and complain…save more money and then go out and buy it. If the world seems unfair, don't complain about it…become someone like Susan B. Anthony, Martin Luther King, or Mother Teresa and do *something* other than whining and complaining. Make a difference in the world in a positive fashion and the world will beat a path to your door. Very few people will become famous like the three I just mentioned, but everyone can make a difference and everyone matters.

Whiners and complainers tend to exude *victim-mentality*. They work in jobs they hate, are married to people they don't love, and they never have enough money for anything they want. They seem to seek out negative situations so that they have something to complain about. They resent rich people, successful people, talented people and good-looking people. They generally believe that those people have some sort of unfair advantage and do not deserve their money, success, fame or attractiveness. Their only joy comes from regaling friends and family members with stories of how badly things have gone for them. It is as if negativity has consumed them and without it they have no strength or purpose. They are lost, sad people and as much as I object to their whining, I pity them for the emptiness of their lives.

If you want to get along with people, remember that whining will cast doubt on any credibility you might have earned from all of the positive acts you have done during your life. It is a destroyer of respect and a killer of relationships.

EIGHTH COMMANDMENT
DON'T BE SELFISH

If you want to get along with people think about someone other than yourself. If you are not getting along with people it is probably largely due to your own actions and the fact that you are thinking more about yourself than the person you are not getting along with.

I once applied for a job as a sales manager with a large, international insurance firm. Part of the application process was a multiple-choice exam to determine the mindsets of the various candidates. I can only recall one question on the exam: *"What is the most important characteristic of a great sales manager?"* There were ten possible answers and I had to rank them from one to ten in order of importance. I got it wrong. I vaguely recall that the answer I chose as number one had to do with market knowledge and the ability to stay in touch with client needs. The actual best answer was, *"The desire to see others do well."* Frankly, I had never observed that selfless trait in any of the sales managers I had known during my career so I did not expect it to be the number one answer. By the way, I did not get the job, but I have never forgotten that one question and its wonderful answer. If you forget the context of the question and just think about a world where everyone has a constant, daily desire to see others do well, you will understand why I cannot get it out of my mind. I have learned that if I put others before myself, I will quite unavoidably bring positive energy to everything I do.

Throughout this book, we have explored relationships and why people have trouble getting along with each other. If everyone spent more time thinking about the hopes, needs, and feelings of others, everyone would get along all the time. Gone would be argument, strife, and dissention. Gone would be divorce, bullying, and envy. Life would truly be good if people would just stop being selfish.

People with no friends have very little desire to see anyone else doing well. They think only about their own existence. People who lose friends usually lose them because they have stopped caring about their needs, choosing to think only of themselves. Wives and husbands who divorce, have stopped caring about each other, instead thinking only about their own needs and wants. Oh and by the way, sales managers who put themselves before their sales people tend not to have their support and ultimately fail to produce good results. If it is obvious that their primary desire is to make themselves successful, their sales people will rebel by doing everything they can to prevent it. The same thing will happen in almost any relationship. Selfish thinking never produces positive results.

NINTH COMMANDMENT
CONTROL YOUR TEMPER

I keep hearing about road-rage in the media. Apparently road-rage is some sort of psychological condition that causes people who operate motor vehicles to become excessively angry and aggressive while maneuvering in traffic. Highly educated psychiatrists, psychologists and behaviorists have spent a lot of time researching this new-age phenomenon. They publish articles on it and discuss it on talk shows. It is blamed for motor vehicle accidents and used as a defense by guilty drivers…oh for God's sake! Road-rage is nothing more than childish, bad behavior!

Competitive, selfish people believe they have a right to the road and that everyone else should get out of their way. While they are behind the wheel they consider themselves expert drivers who are surrounded by amateurs. They seem to believe that all other drivers should be punished whenever they make an error in judgment or, God-forbid, drive too slow. Their windshields protect them from actual contact with their victims and their finger wagging or bird flipping is soon forgotten as they race past at break-neck speeds. They accomplish nothing with their anger other than causing accidents and creating rage or fear in the drivers they accost. As is the case with all anger, road-rage is wasted energy. Oh, and let's not forget that road-rage makes the *rager* appear silly and childish.

Anger in any situation is frightening, confusing, and annoying to those unfortunate enough to witness it. When a person is angry she is exercising her primeval fight or flight response to something that has occurred or which she fears may occur. That response is natural in animals because they do not have adequate intellect to choose between anger and reason. Barking dogs or charging bears act in that manner in order to protect their territory or their families. Their immediate response to any foreign, external stimulus is to take a threatening, angry stance in order to frighten the intruder away. However, even a dog can be trained to avoid anger when threatened. Dog trainers and animal handlers make a living out of teaching animals to control their natural tendency to retaliate against external stimulus. They do this to protect humans and other animals they live and work with. I think we need more trainers in the world for angry human beings because there are still a lot of them among us.

In most cases, when an angry person blows up, they have not thought it through and end up regretting it later. However, there are still some folks in the world that feel justified when they yell at someone or hurt a member of mankind with angry words. Fortunately, most people soon come to the realization that they have acted in a manner that is not acceptable in civilized society. At that point they will either apologize for their wrongdoing or pretend that it never happened. In either case, the damage has been done and their act of aggression will not soon be forgotten. They will be remembered as angry people long after they have passed from this earth. While on this earth, they will be avoided or talked about behind their backs. Whenever you feel the warm flush of anger coming to your face, think about your words and actions before you speak or act. If you want to get along with people remember that anger is the most pure form of wasted human energy and do everything you can to eliminate it from your life.

TENTH COMMANDMENT
BE NICE

As I reach the end of this book, I feel the need to sum up all of the concepts of *"Getting Along With People Is Easy."* If I had to provide a one-sentence summary of this book, I would have to say, *"Just be nice!"* Nice people are happy people and they almost always get along with the people they meet.

Here is one final definition for you. My dictionary defines *nice* as: *Pleasing; agreeable; delightful e.g. a nice visit. Amiably pleasant; kind.*

Synonyms include: *pleasant, good, kind, polite, and fine.* Are you all of these things? Do you fit the definition of nice?

As you move through the years that are your life, try to improve as you go. Today is the first day of the rest of your life and a new beginning can start right now. Try to be nice to everyone you meet and put some genuine effort into getting along with people. Turn the other cheek whenever necessary and go out of your way to understand others. Do yourself the favor of offering kindness to anyone in need whether it is convenient or not. We are all related to each other on this big, blue planet and we have an obligation to be pleasant with everyone we meet. Politeness is easy and being agreeable with everyone is an attainable objective for all people. Despite past disappointments, if you deliberately seek to please everyone who enters your life from now on, you will be a success. You can choose to become a nice person at any time in your life…it is never too late!

Always remember that there are consequences to your actions. If you want good consequences, your actions must be driven by positive energy. Happiness blooms from the power of positivity. The number of happy people in your life will define your success so be nice to everyone you meet and success will follow.

The final words:

Allow every person you meet to become a positive force in your life and you will find that getting along with people is EASY!

What did we learn in Chapter Eleven?

THE TEN "EASY" COMMANDMENTS

1. TAKE RESPONSIBILITY FOR EVERYTHING YOU DO

2. APOLOGIZE SINCERELY

3. EXERCISE PATIENCE

4. ALWAYS SHOW GRATITUDE

5. BRING HUMOR TO EVERY RELATIONSHIP

6. LISTEN WELL

7. DON'T BE A WHINER

8. DON'T BE SELFISH

9. CONTROL YOUR TEMPER

10. BE NICE

The end for me.

A new beginning for you.

Wayne Kehl

www.waynekehl.com

Printed in the United States
139720LV00001B/13/P

9 781438 937236